the Book of Abundance

Money, Power & Love

Also available as an Ebook
ISBN 978-90-78560-10-4

Also available in:
Dutch   978-90-78560-04-3   (paperback)
Dutch   978-90-78560-00-5   (ebook)
German   978-3-00-042852-4   (hardcover)
German   978-3-00-042853-1   (ebook)
Spanish   978-90-78560-08-1   (paperback)
Spanish   978-90-78560-09-8   (ebook)

the Book of Abundance

Money, Power & Love

Sunny Nederlof & Bas Buis

TABLE OF CONTENTS

Part I

Part II

Part III

Part IV

Acknowledgement

We'd like to thank our students and friends for all that we've experienced together. Every event contributed in its own unique way.

We'd also like to thank Rick Nederlof, Peggy Nederlof David Ben-Asher and Jony Bernardy for their support and translation of this book into English.

We appreciate the editorial contribution of our editor, Guus Vlaskamp from Kosmos-Z&K publishers. He truly understands the art of being a detached reader and philosopher, while never losing sight of the power of language and style.

And we would like to thank the guide Argef. Without his wisdom and clear answers the method and the book would not be complete.

In closing we would like to thank you, our reader, for buying and reading this book.

PART I

Introduction; Lack and Abundance

Money Power Love

Where Do you Stand Now?

Review of Your Sentences

About the Laws of Nature

INTRODUCTION

We all understand the meaning of "lack," and we also understand the meaning of "abundance." Even so, very few know how to create abundance in their lives and how to avoid falling into poverty and lack.

If you want to know how to bring abundance into your life, and more importantly how to hold onto it, then Money Power Love may be the most treasured acquisition you have ever made.

Lack and abundance are not "chance" circumstances that happen to you. The word 'chance suggesting you have absolutely no influence, or it all happened through no fault of your own.
Of-course some people have a better or easier start in life than others, but somewhere in their 'timeline' there should be a moment of truth and self-realization, when he or she realizes it's not the past that counts. From that moment onwards the future is decided by conscious thought, and more importantly conscious knowledge of the three laws of nature dealing with money, power and love.

We want you to know that material things and spirituality can absolutely go hand in hand. We would also like to pass on the knowledge that to know the laws of nature, which you will learn one by one, means that you most definitely can change your life! People needn't stay in a familiar world where they feel "safe." Success and abundance is within reach of everyone.

A Journey

We will take you on a journey. An exciting one, about the three laws of nature, which together form the driving force behind the elements that seem to be the undercurrent in everybody's daily lives.

This method brings:

- more abundance in your life
- prepares you to have plenty of money and gives you the necessary tools to use it responsibly
- more power to your life. Power that gives self-confidence to be yourself, and tranquility to promote your health. Power to do what you want, in the way that you want
- more love in your life
- fewer problems related to money, power and love
- power and positive energy that bring new possibilities
- insights into earthly matters, as well as the more spiritual realities of our existence
- better decisions in your life
- insight and knowledge to help others make more conscious choices

There is a connection between love, power and money that you previously never thought possible. Money power love is one of the most spellbinding (and sometimes underestimated) concepts of life.

This books is about the relationship between the three laws of nature governing abundance, which we will share with you later, and the way we all live our lives. Once you really know—and above all feel—how money power love works, you will be able to explain your own past, both your painful and positive memories. Why did this particular thing happen? Why did it happen to me?

There appears to be a direct relationship between the way people handle money, power and love and problems like divorces, troublesome relationships, hopeless love lives, never-ending money problems, crashed economies, bankruptcies, stock market losses, rejected job applications, and even the state of one's immune system. From the very first time we taught the concept and explained the meaning, Money Power Love was a smash hit. The reactions that this way of thinking - in the form of this book - brought about, were totally unforeseen. It led to spontaneous new insights. The substance and insights it brought have helped many, and it has been an eye-opener for many as well.

After reading money power love
your life will never be the same...

MONEY POWER LOVE

These are the three basic elements that make up our society: money, power and love.
Why do they appear together? Why do they also disappear together? Why is it that some so easily acquire more of them than others? We'll discuss the manner in which you, yourself, fortunately can change this. You will see how simple and how exciting it is to use these three basic forms, once you know how.

Money power love is a relatively simple method to apply, but it is not easy when it comes to letting go of "old" ideas and thought patterns that you're used to. The method will sometimes make you angry. We'd like to ask you to continue and not give up. At times it will confront you with events that, after obtaining new insights, you may want to reevaluate as "mistakes."

Know this: there are no mistakes. In fact there are only experiences, and that's why we ask you to continue. The method will sometimes amaze you in its simplicity when it comes to the laws of nature that you'll get to know. There too, we'll ask you to continue and reach further than that, beyond those insights. The book will lead you to deeper insights, which will show you what the three basic forms really are!

Even then we will ask you to continue... to go on living with these joyful and enriching insights! Money Power Love is for everyone who finally wants to know how it really works. Not just by reading about it, or by understanding it, but by adopting a state of mind in which you are able to handle money, power and love even better than before, so that you can easily integrate them, in a more natural and unstressed way, into your daily life.

Practical

Money Power Love is a practical method. It doesn't fall into old cliches like "save and you become rich" or "don't spend more than you earn". No matter how true you think these sayings might be, they fall under the limited scope of thinking that characterizes "old" ways of thinking. This book gives you the possibility to acquire a new, sensitive state of mind, a state of mind with ample room for money, power and love. A place in life that no longer has to be conquered, but that is simply self evident. The method gives you insight. It takes you step by step on an enlightening journey to the universal truth of our existence.

Really understanding money, power and love and applying the method we present you, will enable you to stop struggling through life. It will enable you to live from a state of abundance, which will make it easier to be yourself and enjoy life more.

As you come to understand this material, it will become clear that money, power and love are not difficult or complicated subjects to understand. They are simple and full of life and joy! They are easily understood. Not only are they easy to understand, they are also easily generated!

To live in abundance, be wealthy and feel wealthy, in all aspects of life, is not all that complicated. Like the method we will share with you in this book, it's easy! Everybody can do it. You can do it.

Money power and love goes much further than its internal and external perception and far beyond its societal characteristics

It is about the true meaning of money power love and about the laws of the universe

WHERE DO YOU STAND NOW?

Now it's time to get down to the serious stuff. This is a simple but very important exercise. At the end of this book, and maybe even sooner, you'll come to appreciate this exercise to its fullest. It will become one of the most important and crucial eye-openers in your life.

Exercise:

Put into words how you think about money. How do you feel deep inside when you think about money? Take a moment to think about a sentence that includes the word money and the word I or me.

For example:
I think that money…
Or: Money means … to me.

Make your sentence as short as possible, in any case, no longer than two lines. Take your time and think about it. If more sentences and meanings run through your head, then take the first one that you think of that feels most comfortable to you. There is no need for it to be pretty, well constructed or poetic sounding. Don't worry about what it sounds like or what others expect from you. Write the sentence down, because you'll be needing it.
(Don't read any further before writing it down!)

Space to write down your sentences:

Date: Your name:

Sentence 1

....

....

....

Sentence 2

....

....

....

Sentence 3

....

....

....

Next you'll be changing your first sentence. Write your sentence again underneath the previous one, but with one small change: Leave out the word money, and replace it with the word power. Don't change anything else! Even if the sentence looks strange, sounds strange, is not proper English, or you feel that it does not do justice to you as a person.

Underneath that you'll repeat the same sentence with another small change: Replace the word power with love. Again, do not change anything else. Don't even change or add the most innocent looking word that might have the same meaning just so that it feels right again.

Now take a look at all three sentences. How does the first sentences feel to you? You made it up yourself. There's no denying it came entirely from you.

How does the second sentence feel to you? This one might feel a bit strange and "unreal." You might want to put the blame on us for this second sentence, because if you had known beforehand...

The third sentence might feel even stranger than the previous one. "But that's not the way I think about love at all! Ridiculous! What kind of an exercise is this? As if you could compare money, power and love with each other!"

Don't get too upset. The fact that it feels or looks funny doesn't make it less true! We'll show you that this is exactly what it is all about, and we guarantee that you'll be sharing the exercise joyfully with friends and acquaintances later. However, we advise you to wait until you've read the entire book.

REVIEW OF YOUR SENTENCES

What did you say and how did you feel, now that you have written down all three sentences?

Do you feel really angry and unreasonable? Then you have a sentence in the 1st category:

- I think that money is dirty.
- I think that money is a necessary evil.
- Money is the root of all evil

Are you just slightly angry or indignant? Then you have a sentence in the 2nd category:

- Money is not important to me.
- There are more important things than money.
- Money doesn't buy happiness.
- I'd much rather see a world without money.
- I don't really need money.

Does it give you a confused feeling? Then you are having mixed and conditional feelings, the 3rd category:

- Money is not important to me, but unfortunately it is necessary.

- If I had a choice between money and happiness, I know which one I would pick.
- Money is necessary and handy to have, but absolutely not the most important thing.
- Money doesn't buy happiness, but does make life easier.

Do you have a neutral, unemotional kind of feeling about the sentence? Then you are more in the "dull" state of life, category 4:

- I only need money to live.
- I feel impartial toward money.
- Money doesn't mean much to me.
- Money is only there to spend.
- I only need money to pay the bills.

Maybe you feel some hope and desire for independence, category 5:

- Money buys me freedom.
- To me, money means freedom and ease.
- To me, money means no worries.

Is it a feeling of "it's kind of nonsense," but without emotion or direct rejection of your own sentence? That means "safe emotions" and distance, category 6:

- Money is easy to me.

- Money gives me possibilities.

- Money is no problem for me.

Or do you feel a sense of relief in the sentences? Then you belong in category 7, satisfaction:

- I always have enough money.

- Money in today's times is important.

- I have learned to value money.

And category 8, the last, is that of joy:

- I love money.

- Money is a fantastic part of my life.

- I delight in having money.

Take your time and study the different categories. Which, in terms feelings, comes closest to your sentence? Of course your sentence is unique, but it will fit in somewhere. And, whatever the sentence, don't worry about it! After reading this book you'll have so much insight into money, power and love that your sentence will come to have a whole different meaning. As you start to adopt this way of thinking and being in your daily life, you'll notice that your sentence is nothing but a reflection of your life and that it will change often!

Sometimes it's about one little word and at other times about a whole new sentence.

Once we called a good friend to ask her the same question. Before we called, we were both pretty sure what her answer would be. But she wasn't home, and we got her daughter on the line. During the conversation that ensued, we decided to ask her the same question. She thought it was a good challenge. After the telephone conversation we asked her to have her mom return our call as soon as she got home, and we asked her in particular not to reveal the question beforehand! She promised not to tell, but she thought she could probably guess her mother's answer.

She gave us exactly the same answer that we thought her mother would give!

The meaning of money is so anchored in one's psyche that many people already feel and know how a good friend or parent will answer! That's why there's no point in trying to make your sentence "prettier" than your initial true feeling. Trying to be spiritual, fibbing a little, being ashamed of the meaning, and feeling guilty are all good reasons to want to change your sentence from what you truly feel in your heart. Those around you can sense the truth nonetheless. They are also aware when you say one thing and end up doing something else!

Explanation of category 1

If you said that money is dirty, your second sentence says that power is dirty and the third that love is dirty. We're not going to tell you that that's not the case, because it's always the case. If you said this, it means that you have a particular fixed idea that comes from your attitude about life. It is this belief or conviction that makes it very difficult for you to integrate money, power and love into your life in an easy and loving manner. By saying that money is dirty, you are really saying that you do not want to have it, that you want as little to do with it as possible, and that you're not sure exactly what place to give it in your life. Of course you could deny this. You could call it ridiculous and logically try to explain it away, but if you take the time and truly look at your life, then you'll find it to be true. And so a bit of protest is to be expected.

Explanation of category 2

If your sentence says more or less "I don't really need the money," you may just as well leave out the words really and the. You're left with "I don't need money." In that case, you don't need power. And you don't need love. This sentence points to a state of loneliness. Not necessarily that you have no partner or family, but there is a permanent tendency to distance yourself from money, power and love. You make that distance by working too hard, traveling a lot, or by creating an "impregnable" image.

Explanation of category 3

If your sentence is "money is necessary and handy to have, but it's absolutely not the most important thing in the world," you are in the category of conditionality and choices. This points to a life of preferably playing it safe and the attaching a "what if" to everything. The mere fact that you feel you have to choose between two extremes shows that you don't believe in unconditional abundance, that you are afraid that lightning might strike you as punishment from the gods if you wished for abundance without any limits. These limits will appear in your work and in your relations in the form of holding back and seldom making a choice and going for it.

Explanation of category 4

If your sentence is "I need money to pay my debts in society," that says a lot. It means you have tied certain conditions to money, the most important condition being that money exists only to pay society's bills. If you wrote this sentence, you'll always be left holding the bag. No matter how good you are at earning money, there will always be bills coming in to suck up all your earnings (isn't that what your money was for?). Relations and ex-partners are costing you loads of money, a court case here, a conflict there. If there is an argument in the family, you'll always get or accept the blame. You're usually the one people come to to complain. You are the mediator, and if something goes wrong, it's your fault. Still, you really can't complain, because your second sentence is "I only need power to pay off my debts," and your third sentence is "I only need love to pay off my debts." So it makes sense. But even now you have a choice. You can be thankful that the wishes you wrote down are being fulfilled, or you could at this very moment choose to totally rethink your outlook on money, and therefore on power and love.

Explanation of category 5

If you said "money gives me freedom," in essence you are saying that your freedom depends entirely on the amount of money you have. It also means that you don't feel free and that in a sense you feel dependent. You feel dependent on the amount of money, power and love. By burdening yourself with this feeling of dependence, you are limiting yourself and will always be able to find causes outside yourself that you think are responsible for your present situation. However, this category is a good step towards daring to enjoy.

Explanation of category 6

A sentence like "money is easy" shows that you are well on your way to accepting the energy of money, but that you are holding back in fear of the criticism of others. This will also become apparent in your love life, which will have a tendency toward casualness even though you really know better.

Explanation of category 7

If you said "I always have enough money," it shows clearly that you have no aversion toward the energy of money, power and love and that you posses a measure of trust in life. A bit more joy over this happy fact would definitely be in place.

Explanation of category 8

"I love money" is the most beautiful category you could wish for yourself. Of course, every category can offer magnificent insights, but this sentence is worthy of congratulations! It stands for openness, joy and unconditional acceptance. This enormous degree of trust will be reflected in everything you do and undertake and will be beneficial for all your personal relations!

As you may have noticed, this one sentence of yours about the meaning of money plays a huge role and carries a lot of weight. Even though you may still be in a state of denial, this one sentence lays completely bare how you feel about money, power and love.

In the next chapter, the first law of nature will clearly show the relationship between money, power and love.

ABOUT THE LAWS OF NATURE

Money, power and love function according to three laws of nature. They are consciously called *laws of nature,* because they are natural and they act as laws. They are part of this world and cannot be avoided. They always apply, without exception and to everybody. The beauty is that they are not complicated. They are simple to name, to remember, and more importantly, very easy to apply!

These laws of nature are:

- Money, power and love are one energy
- The energy has to flow
- Energy follows thought

In the course of this book you'll learn about these three laws one by one. We'll also include a number of chapters to clarify them.

PART II

The First Law of Nature: It's All One Energy

The Three Forms

>   Money

>   Power

>   Love

The Energy Can Be Felt

Test Yourself: Signals

The Energy is Boundless

THE FIRST LAW OF NATURE:

Money, Power and Love Are One Energy

The first law of nature is: money, power and love are one energy. It all comes from the same source and answers to the same laws of nature. Of course, money is not the same as power and power is not the same as love. They are, however, only superficially different. *They are three different aspects of one and the same energy.*

We live in a world that has long put the emphasis on differences. As a result, differences have received a lot more attention than similarities. Are you getting antsy yet? Are you starting to distance yourself from this point of view, maybe even getting fidgety in your chair? Are you almost ready to put this book aside?

That's possible. At every moment you have the right, your birthright, to choose your own path in life. Maybe this is the right moment to make a choice. Now, once and for all. Do you feel drawn to a life full of disappointments, full of turmoil, misery and pain, or do you, from now on, wish for a life flowing from the real essence of love, from a feeling of abundance, a prosperous life filled with money, power and love? Our advice is to choose the latter! If you're not able to make a decision at this point without reservation, then decide to give it a try for the rest of this book. Simply try it out, without any obligation! You can always go back to the old ideas and values you had until today, if you so desire. So, it's one and the same energy; that cannot be said often enough.

Accepting this first law of nature will have several consequences.

The way we deal with one aspect, is the way we will deal with the others

That means that if you have a casual attitude toward money, you will also have a casual attitude toward power, and you will also have the same attitude towards love. That nonchalance will be reflected in love relations, business ventures, and even your health.

Someone who hates money will also have difficulty standing up for himself in society and will feel less supported by society. There is a good chance that such a person will deny this, because it doesn't feel that way to him. It has everything to do with one's attitude towards life!

The three aspects go together

It is definitely possible to have money and power and love. You don't have to choose between the three! Often you will hear "money? Just give me health," or "money can't buy happiness." From this moment on, you never have to choose again. Never!

Imagine you're in a situation without money. At the same time your mother is sick and you would be extremely happy if her health would improve. You don't have to feel guilty to admit that having more money would be nice. It's not one or the other. You should know that if you acknowledge that you are entitled to money and power and love, that is what really sets the flow of abundance in motion! In fact, it's the desire to substitute one for the other that throws everything off balance. You cannot substitute one for the other.

Thus, the three forms cannot appear by themselves. They always go together. Money, power and love are three different forms of the same energy. We now know that these three forms are all equally important. If you deny one of them, if you deny that they are one energy, or if you resist this principle, that means you dissipate and reject the energy as a whole.

Of course, you could deny this. Anyone can use words and wonderful theories to negate the value of one of the three forms. Sometimes it may even seem like you've succeeded, but sooner or later the truth comes out. After all, you can't fool the universe, only your perception... You cannot separate the three forms: money, power and love.

Money is not the essential thing;
it is not a necessity

Money is a logical consequence
of your spiritual attitude

THE THREE FORMS OF THE ONE ENERGY

You know now that money, power and love is one energy. But what is money really? What is real power and what is love exactly?

MONEY

Material things, and particularly money, are extremely confrontational. We are using this material element here like a mirror, like a crow bar, to clarify for you something about your convictions and to see where you stand. We'll take money first, because this element is considered the most material of the three. As a result, people, as individuals and as a whole, respond to it in the most basic way. Money is tangible. After all, everybody uses it. You can count money, you can look at it, you can stack it up, save it, carry it, and very easily give it away. It is part of everybody's life in our society, whether or not you accept money as something that brings joy.

The Essence of Money

Did you ever take a moment to think about the real value, the deeper meaning, of money? What is money really? Money is, of course, much more than coins and stacks of bills. Money is the great mirror, the great universal sword of truth. Money reveals people's true nature and how we interact with one another. That doesn't mean money is something to be worshipped or that you should regard it as the most important thing in life. It means only that money should be honored for what it is. It can take you to heaven or to hell. It can give rise to the best in one person and the worst in another.

Physically speaking, money has several characteristics, one of which is that there is no lack in money. There are warehouses full of it all over the world. Money is a piece of paper that has an equivalent value. In fact, money is really an agreement.

Take for example the consolidation of many different currencies into one, as was recently done in the European Union. That was also done in the United States after the Civil War. These are clear and perfect illustrations that money is nothing more than an agreement between people! This is the way money originated. Money was created because of the need for a universal means of exchange that was not seasonal and could not spoil like grain, corn, meat, or vegetables. Money as a means of exchange has the advantage that it is a more direct form of energy. It therefore also has many more possibilities. There is no longer any need to exchange a goat for butter and to exchange that for grain, which is what you wanted in the first place. The old way simply had too many drawbacks.

There are certain groups of people that have such a great aversion to money that they created alternative systems. They realized of course that we could not go back to the time of non-neutral exchange elements like chickens and cocoa beans, so instead they created money substitutes like "credits." At first those money substitutes seemed to fulfill their expectations, but after a while it appeared that some participants were so successful in their exchanges and provision of services that they had enough "credits" saved up to live off for many years to come. Other participants provided services that were not in high demand, and they lived in a state of perpetual lack. Beginning to sound familiar? All of these systems went through the same development as money. The wheel was simply being reinvented over and over again. Money is a natural part of life. Accept it as a loving expression of energy!

Money is simply love, a loving appreciation for each other's services and products

If we look at this energy in the form of money, this loving appreciation is beautifully expressed during all transactions involving money. Perhaps you've been working for years for the same boss and think that this rule does not apply to you. However, every few years the unions conduct negotiations for your salary increase, days off, and other working conditions. Even if you're hardly aware of it, it's done on your behalf. And be honest, you're sure to appreciate the raise! Apparently, we consider it important to earn recognition for what we do in terms of money. Now that you know that it's all one energy, that's also logical. In fact, during those negotiations, what's being discussed is how much your work is appreciated. In other words, how much are you loved as an employee.

Some people find it extremely difficult to accept the fact that it is one energy. They argue that money is so unimportant to them that they've become minimalists. They live simply, prefer to avoid making any purchases, and receive almost everything free by roaming the streets looking for bargains or trades. Their motto is "free or cheap is better!" After all, money is dirty and the less you have to do with it the better. But wait. If their aim in life is to have as little to do with money as possible, in fact they're extremely money oriented. Every time they do, buy, trade or need anything, their aim will be to spend as little money as possible, and if possible not to spend any money at all. In that case they're being too focused on money. That's TOTAL money absorption.

When talking about money, power and love,
it's not about quantity!

Money is Energy

It's a saying that you must have heard or even might have said yourself: money is dirty. Of course, money as a material isn't dirty. It's only paper with an imprint that somebody designed and nothing else. The same holds true for coins. A piece of metal with an imprint. Coins and paper money are really nothing but an agreement. Money is energy. Energy is just energy and can't be dirty.

Money is a materialization of intention

With money you can buy all kinds of nice things. You can support good causes with your money. Whatever you might think about it, they're happy to receive it and rightly so. With money you can support your family and help friends in times of need. Whether you see money as paper without a soul or, like us, as a form of energy, it can't do anything of its own accord. It can't walk over and drop itself in the Red Cross collection box. It doesn't take itself to drug dealers. It is literally done by the hands of the people that do it, sent or guided by their intentions. So every good or bad deed is motivated by thought, the intention, the justification, the fears, the unspoken need behind the act.

Money is wonderful

Having money feels great. It gives you a feeling of being loved, and it gives you a feeling of safety. It lets you feel that there is a place for you in this world and that there is a need for what you do and produce. It is well known that in neighborhoods where everyone has "enough" money there is less trouble with aggression and that folks in these districts are usually healthier and live longer.

Money needs love

We don't trade things like grain or animals. We now have another means of exchange and think that it doesn't need to be cared for, that it doesn't need love. Nothing could be further from the truth! Money comes to you willingly only if you handle it with love, just like a dog or cat. Dogs or cats don't go willingly to people who don't love them, and if they do they usually don't stay long or they become sick because of lack of attention and love and just wither away. It will help you if you integrate money in a loving manner into your life and care for it with love. And we mean that more literally than you may think.

Realize that the way you treat money

is also the way you treat power and love!

Exercise

Start with the decision, from now on, to be really nice to money. You can do this simply by consciously being happy whenever you receive money from someone. Truly happy! Not like it's just something that happened to come into your life, but receive it with the same love that you would bestow on a baby or a puppy. Be consciously delighted every time it comes your way, every time you receive your paycheck, when you find a dime on the street, or when you get paid by a client. Also, always be very conscious of the giver. Be conscious of what he gives, the reason it is given, and thank him for it in a manner that is clear. Be consciously aware that not only money came your way, but also power and love. After all, it's one energy.

But wait. That also means being nice to money when you pay your bills! Realize what you are paying for, what you have received for it, and be really happy from your heart that you are able to pay this bill! Pay with concentration, with involvement, sincerity, and love. Do that when you eat out in a restaurant, in the supermarket, when you pay the rent, and even when you pay a speeding ticket. And just like when you receive, be consciously aware of the other party. Be aware who you give the money to and recognize their right to receive it. Clearly say "please" and "thank you," and dare to take the time to do so, rather than mumbling a bit in the hope it wasn't really heard. And finally, look the person in the eyes! Dare to make contact on a deeper level, even if it is about a quarter or "just" a penny.

POWER

Power feels much less earthly than money. It seems much more vague, and unlike money you can't really look at it close up, feel it, count it, or save it. Nobody really knows what it looks like, but we genuinely feel whether someone "has it" or "doesn't."

Many people have strange ideas about power, varying from being macho to acting tough. That applies to both men and women. If we look at the mental level, it seems that ideas about power range from control to soft persuasion, to even light manipulation (euphemistically called "being guided") amidst the network of friends and business relations. No matter how these appearances seem to be part of people's lives, none of them have anything to do with power, only with fear.

What is power really? We need power in our lives. We need it if we're trying to reach a goal in life. Power is one of the ingredients needed to achieve what we want to achieve, to be a cause rather than a victim of circumstance. But power goes much further. True power gives us physical as well as spiritual health. It ensures that we not only feel strong, but that we truly are strong. With true power we can confront the world in a positive way, instead of having to struggle. Believe us, struggle isn't necessary!

Power is life without struggle

Real power is the absence of manipulation, of force and mental blackmail. Power is not a thing. It is not something you 'do'. It is a state of being. It is something you are, just like money is a state of being.

Power you feel deep inside

True power is love. True power is complete self acceptance and the resulting ability to feel complete and unconditional love for others. True power is a state of being that exists the moment you stop criticizing or belittling yourself. Honestly, to be truly powerful from every fiber of your body and mind is wonderful. When you are "in power," you will really feel strong. You'll feel energetic and open to everyone. You won't feel threatened by anyone or anything.

Power is the most beautiful thing there is. Experiencing power gives you the chance to shine like the sun. The best thing about power is that as soon as you experience it, you become a model for others. Being powerful gives others a conscious - and especially an unconscious - license to emulate you and be powerful too. To have inner strength enables you to help others when they need help, no matter how! You can share your strength with them.

Man cannot live without strength and thus not without power either. It's not just by chance that we know the words weak and powerless and in contrast to *be in charge* and to have *power over your own life*. Power comes from what you are and who you are and is not an end in itself. An exaggerated amount of power resulting from force rather than from strength is the consequence of fear and implies a very strong wish for control. In that case power is used intentionally. Real strength leads towards power and thus requires an enormous amount of responsibility. The fact that some are just not competent handling this responsibility has got nothing to do with the nature of power.

Power is not force

True power comes straight from love and from trust. Power is letting loose of being result-oriented and letting go of control without belittling yourself. Force, on the other hand, arises from fear and wants to control. Might is ego; might is result-oriented and makes you tired.

Power makes you visible

Even though it is less tangible, energy in the form of power is just as confrontational as the energy of money. Many people push away the energy of power before they can truly realize and experience the beauty of it. At some time in their lives they experience a small sample of what power is and then run away from it as hard as they can.

Why is that? At the beginning, being engulfed by power or being in a state of power can be a frightening experience. Once you start to experience power in your life, you aren't anonymous anymore. You lose your "invisibility" in society. If you're in a state of power, you feel for the first time in your life what it means to bear full responsibility and also what it means to be able to bear it. In the beginning that can feel a little scary, sometimes so scary you forget that by being powerful you could make use of the related rules belonging to power. Because power has something quite beautiful within it; the whole world will open up to you when you are powerful. When you are powerful, you'll feel like you're alive. You're visible to your surroundings and to the world. Doors suddenly open, fears fall away, and you'll go further than ever seemed possible.

Succeeding versus fear of failure

It's important to know that many people are afraid of failing. But even more people suffer from a lesser-known phenomenon: fear of success. That's the fear to succeed, the fear of becoming noticed, the fear of standing out above the rest. It's actually very simple to get rid of this fear: get used to being in a state of power!

Get used to that strange feeling!

People find it frightening to be noticed or to be singled out. As every actor, every businessman or business-woman, and every politician knows, it can be very scary to have the spotlights aimed at you for the very first time and to feel like everything depends on you. It can be frightening when everything you say and do will be seen and heard by millions of people and that there's absolutely nobody you can hide behind. Later, that's just the daily work of an actor, teacher, businessperson or politician. As soon as they become powerful, the feeling of fear, the fear of being noticed and having the complete attention of the public, vanishes. That's getting used to power. It's actually getting used to literally standing in the spotlight!

A lot of people may think that this way of handling power is only meant for some people. It's true, you may have to get used to the fact that you are just as special, just as powerful, as the president or that sexy movie star or pop star. But to be truly powerful doesn't depend on who you are or what you do. It's a question of performing your work with power, with loving attention, without fear of failing. Power will enter your life if you say and do everything without reservation! This technique of learning to handle power is not meant exclusively for the above-mentioned "noteworthy occupations" in our society; it's for everyone! It is important for anyone who wants more money, power and love in his life to get used to power—a life full of power and self-confidence, sparkling, full of compassion and empathy, without sacrificing your goals or your humanity. Wouldn't that be wonderful?!

Many people have the tendency to avoid this confrontation with themselves. Just know that by avoiding power, knowing that it is one and the same energy, you'll be avoiding money and love as well. They go together. You can't avoid any one of them without avoiding them all.

The more you stand for who and what you are, the more powerful you are and the more you'll be appreciated!

Although money and love are in and of themselves sensitive matters, for many people power is an even bigger problem. People may not talk about it much, but that doesn't mean it's any less important. The truth is, there are very few really powerful people. If you truly are in that state of power, you stand up for yourself and for what you are, like your opinions about politics, about God, about love, and about money. You stand for what and who you are, while at the same time respecting others' full worth and their space to be themselves. To be fully in power and stand for what and who you really are doesn't mean that everybody will always be happy about it. Instinctively, it seems that the more power you have, the less support you may think you're getting from others.

How is it that being powerful is so scary? Because it's new, because taller trees catch more wind and you're afraid of how your friends, family, and colleagues might react. It's true that people often support each other's "dependency," and if one of the parties stops, that can be confrontational for the other.

Power is a stimulating energy

True power is loving. It's a state of mind in which our ego— and thus our tendencies to hold on to our self-image—doesn't count anymore. It's a state of mind in which we always dare to be ourselves, even though we may not know what it will bring. It's a state of mind in which we're not afraid that others might take away our power, because we know that it comes from inside and can never be taken away!

You can accept power

The great thing is that every person has enough power. We have a huge, overwhelming abundance of it if we accept it! You can teach yourself to do this. Every time you feel like you're losing your power, for instance during a conversation or a confrontational situation, ask yourself why that is. Know, and feel deep inside, that you have enough power and just allow it to flow. Power can never be depleted. There is no such thing as a power bank. You can't be in the red! In essence you don't have to do anything for it. It's already part of who you are.

True power is positive

The following technique allows you to efficiently use your power, in other words to control it. Decide that as from NOW, you're going to be consciously aware of how you handle power. You alone decide what you use your power for.

To use your power well, it's necessary to know something about power as a form of energy. The whole world consists of energies. Even human "powers" in society are nothing but energy! Energy can carry two types of charges within itself. One is positive, and the other is a blocking charge. The positive charge ensures that you're always in balance with everything around you, while the blocking charge makes your life more difficult and blocks the flow of money, power and love.

Are you against discrimination? That's very noble, but it is costing you a lot of energy. Does that mean we can all decide that it's okay to discriminate from now on? Of course not. But every thought, every idea that is *against something*, and is therefore costing you energy, can be transformed into something that you are in favor of. Once you know what you are *for*, the energy flowing through you feels as strong as the energy generated when you were against something, but this is the positive version... Ask yourself: What am I actually for? For equality maybe? Or do you feel more comfortable with "we are all one?" You will quickly come to realize that to be for something you have to really contemplate what it is you're for, rather than just being against everything. (Every adolescent can do that...) As soon as you know what you're for, in your heart and soul, you'll have transformed your energy field to a powerful stream that flows with life and that gives you energy, rather than one that sucks your energy away.

For some people, the fact that *to be for something* is totally different than to be *against something* seems confusing. They might think that that to be *for something* automatically means you're against something else. But if you're for peace, you're occupied only with peace and peaceful thoughts. As soon as you allow thoughts or feelings of being against war or anger within your system, you're occupied with war and the energy of peace will disappear out of your system. Mother Theresa lived her life according to this peace-loving principle. If someone invited her to a demonstration that was against something, they received a short response stating that she would not come. But if she was invited to attend a demonstration that was for something, there was every chance that she might show up or support it.

Are you against possessions? Do you feel an overwhelming sense of injustice in your gut if people possess a lot? Do you immediately get the urge to tell these people that all their possessions are really superfluous and that there are a lot of other needy folks who could use them much more? Or do you suffer in silent disgust? If your ideal world is one that brings welfare for everyone, then start by respecting the people who have already obtained it and be happy for them, no matter how difficult that may sometimes be. We invite you to change your feelings to something you can be for instead of against. For instance: "Everybody is entitled to a wonderful life" or "I wish each and every person an abundance of money, power and love."

The question that many will raise is, what about the multitudes of poor people in countries where they live in abominable conditions, and those who are victims of corruption and oppression. Should they just accept their lot and remain victims of their oppressors?

Wishing abundance for everyone is not the same as allowing others to oppress you. The catch is when you get angry at the oppressor and become negative about (their) abundance. People even think that the stream of negativity that this generates has something to do with standing up for oneself or self-empowerment. Unfortunately that is not the case; the angrier you are, the more you contribute to the wealth, power and happiness of the oppressor and the poorer you become. Every time you accept the role of victim, you're giving away your power to someone else. And as soon as you lose power, you'll also lose money and love. You understand that now, and time has proven it to be true. By recognizing others' right to abundance and deciding for yourself, or even better *knowing* that you are entitled to just as much abundance and that you as a person are worth just as much, you will break the cycle.

Not being conscious of these natural laws is the reason why the poor become poorer and the rich become richer. They're being suppressed, emotionally, financially and economically, and their fury and powerlessness only grows. If someone who feels oppressed and powerless responds from a place of power instead of powerlessness, no matter how difficult that might be in a miserable situation, these relations change.

That means not only power in place of powerlessness but also power in place of resignation, without the destructive power of anger. Because no good can ever come from anger and denial, such cooperation between people is doomed to fail. Jealousy of one's oppressor leads to discontentment towards others - towards your neighbors, employers, and even those that have it just a little better than you. That leads to even more divisiveness and increases the power of those you resent. That happens very often, and it's been proven not to work.

People just love the idea of guilt and are totally enslaved to the impulse to lay blame on anything and everything except themselves. If there have been financial abuses and the poor are the ones who suffer, we tend to blame money. If we have a lovers' quarrel, we blame love. We are disappointed in love. To blame one of the three forms of the one energy is the same as polluting a river and then laying the blame on the water.

To blame one of the forms money, power or love doesn't solve anything

Why is it that being against something can feel so good? Being against something not only allows you to express your emotions, it also strengthens and fosters them. For example, emotions like dissatisfaction, aggression, and powerlessness. Releasing such emotions is healthy, but it's best to find another way of doing so. Athletic activities, watching a scary movie, going for a walk, or writing are all much healthier ways of getting out what's inside.

Think of something that you are against, like drugs, criminality, war, or something lighter like annoying neighbors or people who don't clean up after their dogs. Visualize it in front of you. Imagine how they are ruining your world and making it unlivable. Foster that feeling for a few minutes and think of how horrible these people are that won't see eye to eye with you. The adrenaline is flowing through your veins; in a manner of speaking you could hit the streets and protest or send an angry letter to the municipality. This "against" feeling is your signal that you're giving away your energy. It's that simple to awaken and foster a feeling within oneself that instantly stops the flow.

This important principle works for all people at all times. There are no exceptions. To be against something breaks your contact with the positive life flow, while to be for something brings you in contact with that flow and ensures that you are part of it!

And that's only logical. By being against something, you're condemning people and their acts. Be honest, who likes to be condemned? That only crates opposition and enmity, of which you will ultimately be the victim.

You are a child of God

Our deepest fear is not that we are inadequate.
Our deepest fear is that we are powerful
beyond measure.
It is our light, not our darkness that most frightens us.
We ask ourselves, Who am I to be brilliant,
gorgeous, talented, fabulous?
Actually, who are you not to be?
You are a child of God.
Your playing small does not serve the world.
There is nothing enlightened about shrinking so that
other people won't feel insecure around you.
We are all meant to shine, as children do.
We were born to make manifest the glory of God that is
within us. It is not just in some of us; it is in everyone.
And as we let our own light shine, we unconsciously
give other people permission to do the same.
As we are liberated from our own fear,
our presence automatically liberates others.

1992 - Marianne Williamson
A Return To Love: Reflections on
the Principles of A Course in Miracles

LOVE

Love is the most vague of the three forms of the one energy. Love, to be loving, to be found lovely, to be in love, to be loved. All are forms in which love appears. Love is or can be an very important part of our lives. We use the word, we give meaning to it, and we know that we are greatly in need of it. Love stirs up a lot in people. The whole concept of love is actually one of life's most vital questions, and the answer is completely different for every person. If you look around and regularly contemplate life, you'll certainly have noticed that people have a lot of strange ideas about love. Do you already know what love is?

We can meet someone and in one second we can feel deep inside that this is Mister or Miss Right, only to discover shortly thereafter that we were completely wrong. We are able to spend years in a relationship and even live with someone and yet regularly ask ourselves if that person really loves us.

Love can intuitively be an almost "intellectual" joining of two people, in which two individuals strengthen one another in the masks that they have both worn for years. Together they seem to feel stronger than alone, and they strengthen each other's "masks," the ego, in order to avoid change.

Love is sometimes experienced as a completion in our lives, as if without a partner you were not complete and were missing out on something important. Of course having a partner is wonderful, but you have to find your own inner happiness first; otherwise having a partner becomes more of a battle.

For many, the idea of love is just an extension of sex. They don't see sex as the result of love between two people—they see it the other way around! They make a division in their minds between love and sexuality. That enables them to build the illusion of a relationship, including the physical intimacy, without having to give all and open up at a deeper level.

Others see love not only as the very highest and most beautiful thing on earth, but also as something far beyond their reach. It is so holy, so heavenly, and they feel like they are so plain and insignificant, that they believe that love is not for them. Their image is of a prince on a white horse, a knight in shining armor or a beautiful damsel in a castle, longing and forever waiting. People hope, fantasize, and read about it, but deep inside they feel that it's unreachable. They don't realize that the greatest gift on earth is theirs for the taking. Their striving for the "unreachable" makes it invisible.

Love is irreplaceable

This might sound strange to you, but many people are scared to death... of love, to love something or someone, to fall in love, scared of love in many forms. We either attach very mundane implications to love, or we give it a very high, unreachable connotation, instead of simply, without reservation, allowing it into our lives. That gives rise to widespread addiction to the "substitutes" for true love.

The first, and often used, substitute is the need to be recognized. Recognition through hard work or recognition by completely living up to your parents' wishes or expectations. Recognition through success. The need to be recognized is a widespread phenomenon. You can see it clearly among many young people everywhere in the world. The fact that they don't feel recognized as human beings, don't feel loved by society, leads to an extraordinary need to be recognized. Everyone tries to fill that need differently. In one family they might see you as worthy if you, like them, become an artist and have an exhibition at a famous museum. In another milieu you'll receive recognition when you drive a certain type of car or when you are able to purchase your own home. In yet another environment certain forms of intimidation and force will get you respect from your friends. All of these are substitutes for the feeling and experiences of love.

Many so-called substitutes are compulsive addictions and impulses, such as drugs, stimulants, gluttony, working too hard, or even cheating on your partner.

Fortunately, we are living in a wonderful time - a time in which we can free ourselves from expectations from our surroundings and our expectations of ourselves, a time in which we can free ourselves from the substitutes for love.

Love is unconditional

One trap that many fall into when developing and nourishing love is to unconsciously attach certain conditions to love. You become inclined to love only people who love you in return. As soon as you find that they are criticizing you for who you are, for your beliefs or your schooling, you feel resistance and tend to pull back. True love goes further than to love only those who love you. Love is loving everyone, as fellow human beings, even if they criticize you. That doesn't mean that you should surround yourself with such people, but it is important to think about them lovingly and to deal with them in a loving manner whenever your paths cross. It also doesn't mean that you have to compromise your values. Expressing your values with love is fantastic. Just be honest and realize that sparing people's feeling and hiding the truth have nothing to do with love. Show the world that your values actually spread love! By being loving. *Be love!*

You will recognize true love in yourself and in others. Love shines in a person's eyes. You can feel it with every touch. It's visible in daily life when you are honored as a human being, no matter what you do or who you are. Love always has the promise of honesty in it. It never criticizes. Love's aim is always for something and never against.

Everything is love and love is in everything

Love is much less demanding than you may think. People who exist in a state of love are much happier, much healthier, and can tolerate failures much better.

You reach a state of love as soon as you dare to speak out loud the sentence love is in everything, and to totally accept it without reservations of any kind. Love is in everything. It is in your house, in your car, in your keys, in your porch, your cup of tea, and also in you. You can allow love into your life by performing every act with love and thus with your full attention. Then you not only experience love but you are love, in every cell of your body.

If you can't yet feel that love is in everything, start with a decision. Right now, at this very moment, decide to be loving with yourself and others and to undertake everything with your full attention, even though you might not know how to do it. You can practice this very easily. Before you get into your car give it a loving stroke, no matter how strange it may feel at the beginning. If you drive your car for thousands of miles to your vacation destination and back, you can thank the car for it. When you come home, look around and be thankful for your living environment, for the roof over your head. Maybe you own an old clunker of a car; even that deserves love. Be happy with your faithful vehicle and honor it for services rendered.

Up to now we have mentioned a number of larger things, but this principle also applies to the little things in your life. Preparing a delicious cup of coffee and drinking it with love, really with your full attention, enjoying the smell and each sip, is an act of love. Prepare your meal attentively, with love.

This principle can also be applied to relationships. Your relationship with your partner and children for instance. Be thankful for your partner. Honor your partner and honor your children. Carry this attitude over to your work. When you perform your job with joy, when you feel love for your work surroundings, for your colleagues and your clients, it will be much more fulfilling and you'll find yourself entering into a wonderful new period in your life, filled with money, power and love. Love is energy, as are money and power. And energy can be awakened. You can generate it in any quantity and at any moment!

The power of love

The power of love—and in this case love through creating and fostering loving thoughts—is sensational. Having loving, positive thoughts is literally healing. That's a fact. Every thought creates energy and, as you know, there is positive energy and negative or blocking energy. Every positive thought comes from love and brings love with it. A positive lifestyle brings more love in your life. It ensures that you'll have more positive thoughts, and as a result you will experience more love in your life. It's a cycle that grows stronger and stronger. Just as despair creates more despair, love brings forth more love.

THE ENERGY CAN BE FELT

Money, power and love are energy. And energy can be felt. Others can actually feel how you think about the forms of the energy. More people can feel that than you think. When we say feel, we don't mean that someone actually has to touch you or that they look at you with x-ray glasses. We're talking about a way in which we feel each other out as human beings. Everybody experiences this on an unconscious level.

That is clearly recognizable in our daily lives. Somebody starts a business or buys a home, wants to take out a loan from a bank, and gets turned down. The complaint is then very often that the bank employee was being arbitrary or didn't really consider the applicant as a person. Well, guess what? Often they know exactly what they're doing! Of course, the figures and your income play a role, but there is another factor that is at least as important: the other person's sense of how you handle money, power and love. The person who handles your loan application and listens to your story, listens to much more than the words. That makes sense of course, because how can somebody pay back a huge amount of money if he or she isn't able to handle this energy, in this case in the form of money.

The same holds true for power and love. If somebody isn't able to handle or control his power during the conversation about that specific loan, or if the person is overly suspicious and obviously has a distorted relationship with the idea of love and with society in general, how can that person handle this energy in a healthy manner, in this case in the form of money?

Money, power and love also clearly play a role in job interviews. You enter the room, sit down, and have a very short period of time in which to sell yourself. Sometimes you get the feeling that within a couple of minutes the decision has been made, and you feel like you were shortchanged. You get all kinds of ideas about "not being given a chance," of being judged and even discriminated against, and you feel really lousy about it. The first secret is that the judgment really is there. The second secret is that it usually doesn't take two minutes to make that judgment, but only one second: the second you open the door and walk to the chair.

The bank employees and personnel managers with whom we spoke and who participated in our workshops were much more spiritual than you may think. They reluctantly admitted that they usually knew right away who would receive the loan and who wouldn't, that they knew right away who would be hired for a particular position and who wouldn't. Actually, they do their work very well if we use the laws of money, power and love as a guideline. They sense exactly how you think about money, power and love. If you think that money is dirty or that money is a necessary evil, you radiate that attitude. If you think, "O my God, that's a lot of money, I'll never get it," you project that. The bank employee senses something indefinable and immediately wonders whether you're someone who has enough power to repay the loan. And be honest, would you lend money to someone who hates money? How is that person ever going to earn or save enough of what he hates to pay you back? Would you "lend" love to someone who hates love? How is that person ever going to generate enough energy to let it flow back in your direction and repay his "debt?" That is exactly what happens. Someone who has difficulty with money, power and love and still wants to borrow some of something he doesn't like; someone who is looking for a job for which he in any event needs power, while he is not yet able to summon up love for his boss, his salary, his colleagues, and himself; other people sense all of that.

They are all linked

If you experience conflict, denial, or inner doubt with respect to one of the three forms, that doesn't necessarily mean that the experience will be limited to that particular form. In fact, "not being ready" with respect to one of the forms often leads to an disbalance in the other two. For instance, inner doubt about money or even denying the great importance of money often leads to loss of power and even to health problems. The inability to generate real inner strength can lead to an inability to obtain money and love easily.

SIGNALS

There comes a time in the lives of many people when their affairs aren't running as smoothly as they might like. That can involve money, power, or love.

The following are some illustrations that point to a disturbance in the balance of money, power and love. Even though these situations are usually experienced as unpleasant, they can teach you a lot about your life at that moment and are clear signals that you can learn to use.

Unexpected Bills

Some may already know it but that doesn't make it any less true: when unexpected and—especially—big unexpected bills arrive, the balance is clearly off. It's a simple fact that it's not only money that's slipped through your fingers, but also power and love.

Business Is in Decline

When business is in decline, it's time to examine how you handle power and how you handle love. Is the business and every employee empowered? Is the business still being run with love? Do you go to work every day with love? Do you get up each day happy to go to work? Of course it's possible for a business to go sour without it being your "fault," but why do you still work there? Why do you still feel at home at a company with the wrong kind of energy or where the energy is lacking? Know that love and loyalty are not the same as blind faith and fanaticism.

Fines

Being fined stands for aggression, haste, and the experience of being thwarted. If you get all worked up, if you're fighting traffic, fighting the world, and if you go beyond your own and other people's boundaries, a fine is a warning. Fines are the confirmation of unreasonableness, injustice, powerlessness, and unfairness that you're experiencing at that moment in your life. Everything that you experience inwardly, and what you don't yet see or don't want to see, comes out in another form.

More Generally

Take a look as to how you really handle money. Are you fearful or greedy? Do you dare to ask enough for your services, or do you ask too much out of frustration? Why do you keep losing money lately, or on the other hand why has business been so good? When you answer these questions, know that you're handling power and love the same way.

If money doesn't give you a clue, take a look at how you handle power. Are you daring to allow yourself to be empowered lately? Do you dare to make decisions and take responsibility for your life? Are you able to stimulate others to be empowered, or do you think that might undermine your own situation? Love is also a way to obtain insights into your life at this moment. If there is doubt in love, there is doubt in every molecule of your being, and that doubt returns in all three forms.

If you aren't sincerely happy with the arrangements in your daily life, that will be reflected as a lack of power and a lack of money. You may be able to temporarily hold on to what you have and live off of it for a while, but the flow, and thus the movement of money, power and love, will eventually come to a standstill. If you don't feel like getting up in the morning anymore, if you don't get a real sense of satisfaction when you get your salary, if your partner's presence doesn't bring you happiness but only a sense of security, then you definitely have a money-power-love problem. If you don't change things, you'll lose all three.

Of course, the idea is not to let it get that far! In our daily lives, these signals are our greatest gift. They are the mirror of our inner being and of our lives in general.

THE ENERGY IS BOUNDLESS

On one of our journeys to the Far East, we found ourselves on a small island. So small that, at the time, it was hardly inhabited and totally unknown by the tourist masses. Close to the beach there was a little restaurant or more like a food stall that was run by a couple. Every time we walked by, we saw how it radiated harmony. One of them lay peacefully napping or smiling warmly at customers, while the other prepared the most delicious dishes. When their child came home after school, he crawled onto his daddy's stomach and they played and had a wonderful time. It was a joy to order food from them—at a place like that you obviously consumed much more than food.

A couple of weeks later we saw a similar restaurant, but this one radiated poverty. The same kind of restaurant, the same corrugated tin roof, the same kind of family, the same kind of food. But these people looked at their clients totally differently. Their eyes were filled with envy, asking themselves why they were stuck living there. We never went there again.

Two very similar situations. According to the laws of society, they had the same opportunities and the same lack of opportunities. Nevertheless, one situation was full of love and the other was not. And you could really see it: one of the restaurants was much busier than the other. When one of us later taught English at the local school, we saw that the child from the loving environment learned with pleasure, with sparkling eyes, full of curiosity for whatever this beautiful world held in store. Money power love illustrated itself in that situation.

You can find similar situations in every major city and every small town. It's about more than just the amount of money, power and love. It's also about the way we handle the energy.

PART III

THE SECOND LAW OF NATURE:

IT HAS TO FLOW

The first law of nature was that money, power and love are one and the same energy. The second law of nature is that this one energy is always in movement. It "flows." Money, power and love are constantly in motion. As you now know, we're talking about energy, and the three forms are nothing but energy in motion. The whole world is in motion. If we examine any matter with a neutron microscope, even your couch, your car, and your bed are perpetually in motion. There's no such thing as standing still. We can perhaps slow things down, we can attempt to stop a particular process, but an actual standstill is impossible.

Our bodies work the same way. We breath in, we use oxygen, rid our body of other gasses, and breath out. We receive, we use, and we pass it on again. Electricity works the same way. All energies answer to the same law of nature: electricity flows from the socket to a lamp, the lamp uses the electricity and spreads its light. Afterwards, it flows back to the socket and the circuit is completed. If one of the three elements of the circuit is missing, the whole flow stops. It's all about receiving, using, and passing on.

The laws of nature governing receiving, using, and passing on can be applied to money, power and love. It's important to be able to receive money, use it and enjoy it, and then to pass it on to someone else. The same holds true for power. You should be able to receive it without feeling burdened, be able to enjoy it, and then also be able to pass it on to the other people around you. Love answers to the same laws of nature. Receive it with love, enjoy it without fear of running out, and dare to pass love on to the next.

RECEIVING

To really be able to receive is an art. Just as it's impossible under the laws of nature only to receive and not to give, it's an illusion that you can keep giving forever without receiving. "I like to give, but I'm not good at receiving." It might be possible for a short period of time but in the long run it depletes your energy system, and that's never a good thing.

You can only pass on
if you are able to receive

You can learn how to receive. One daily experience that can teach you how is compliments. How do you handle compliments? If somebody were to say to you "that's a nice sweater," how would you respond?

Would you answer:
a "Oh, I've had it forever."
b "It was cheap."
c "Do you really think so?"
d "Thank you!"

This also happens at work. A client thanks you and says "great job!"
What do you say?

a "I was just doing my job."
b "Oh, it was nothing special."
c "Do you really think so?"
d "Thank you! Glad to do it!"

If you find a, b, or c fit you best, then you definitely have a receiving "problem." Only d) means thanks for the compliment; all the others rest are means to avoid (real) receiving.

What you are actually doing when you say thank you is giving thanks that the energy has come your way. That's not customary for many people and some cultures. Giving is considered so commonplace that thanking is looked upon as superfluous. Of course giving is obvious for the giver, but thanking should be just as normal for the receiver. Why shouldn't you say "thanks!"

To be able to receive with your heart and with a real "thank you" is very important. People with a receiving and thus a thank-you problem have an energy problem, and that expresses itself through all three forms. It leads to a money, power and love problem. This applies not only to individual people but also to families, societies, and governments. In cultures where people don't say thank you and where people don't really dare look the giver lovingly in the eye, there is such a massive receiving problem that there is a permanent state of lack. Of course, that state of lack will always lead to a power problem. They always go hand in hand! This is a very important cause of today's poverty and it occurs in precisely those countries where there is a huge gap between the rich and the poor. If we look deeper, we usually find that these are also the cultures and countries where many people work without truly feeling love for their work. On our journeys through the Far East, through Central and South America, and through several African and Middle Eastern countries, we clearly perceived a massive receive-and-give problem. That means the flow of energy slows down considerably, until it finally stagnates. This in turn will always affect the local economy. When the flow "stagnates," people say there is an economic problem. Just like in the west, sadly enough it is usually the poor and "hopeless" layers of society that suffer the most. Products and services without love are not wanted, and people don't want to pay for them. Thus the circle is complete.

When are you able to be truly thankful from deep within your heart and when aren't you? Every time you feel opposition within yourself when thanking somebody, for whatever reason, that says a lot about yourself. Do you feel inferior when you give thanks? Or do you feel superior and artificially hold onto that feeling by not saying thanks? As if you're inferior to the other person if you offer thanks. Thanking someone has nothing to do with positions, with rich or poor, or with being successful or unsuccessful. Giving thanks is about respecting the giver, the giving, the ability to receive, and the energy itself.

Actually, by saying *thank you*, you're saying:

Thanks for the money,
it's great that your spending it here

Thanks for the cooperation, for the help.
Your strength gives me strength

Thanks for your love. I'm glad to receive it and I'm
happy that you're giving it to me

More generally, you are actually giving thanks for the fact that this loving flow of energy, the flow of money, power and love, is flowing your way!

Wanting to Be Liked

Another aspect of having difficulty receiving is wanting to be liked. It's the "please think I'm nice" syndrome. Every beginning therapist, every person starting their own business, and everyone in paid employment who negotiates independently over their salary and work conditions is confronted with this. Being able to receive also means knowing what you're worth as an employee or as a freelancer, knowing what your services and products are worth. Knowing that you're worth a lot as a human being. In fact, it's all the same. A person with low self-esteem will never dare ask what he or she is truly worth and will always meet people who will think exactly the same.

Remember: there will always be enough players and situations that will confirm your self-image

If you can't receive, things go wrong. A therapist who doesn't charge anything in order to "help his patients" will ultimately lose all his patients. That's only logical; patients don't want to be helped by someone with a receiving problem. They want to be helped by someone who has total command over the matters involving money, power and love, and thus also over the flow of this loving energy. They are actually looking for someone who is "in the flow" as we call it. That applies to therapists, spiritual teachers, businessmen and businesswomen, parents, managers, athletes, and artists. When you're in the flow, you're able to communicate your knowledge and your love, to share them with others around you. That's the reason why many think that high-priced products and services are "better." That's why we tend to treat people differently if they hold highly paid positions.

Receiving Comes from Love

You have to receive with a feeling of love. You're open to the world, you know your value, and you have an intuitive feeling for ethics and how to deal with others. Receiving distinguishes itself from fear of lack and therefore constantly needing more.

It is sometimes difficult to know whether you do something because it seemingly is coming your way in the form of money, power and love or because you ended up in a state of fear. But that distinction isn't actually that difficult to make. If a close family member offers to let you buy their house for a great price, that's an act of love. Subletting your state-subsidized apartment for five times the actual rent when you haven't even lived there for years isn't an act of love, because you got that subsidized apartment for a different reason. You changed its purpose even though it wasn't yours, and you received energy in the form of money even though you didn't carry the responsibility for the object itself. If you receive an inheritance, that's an act of love. To curry favor with your uncle in the hope he'll leave you something is of course an act of fear. To accept sick leave benefits when you're sick for a month is simply accepting the flow of money, power and love that's coming your way. If you're receiving disability benefits while you're actually able to work, even though you may have to change fields, is fear. Getting married is an act of love; getting married without reporting it because you are afraid you'll suffer tax consequences or lose your benefits is an act of fear. Money received out of fear only gives a material illusion but doesn't bring happiness or true abundance.

These expressions of fear surface because of a feeling of lack. That feeling of "lack" can manifest itself in many different forms, such as not being able to cope with work pressures, fear of the future, being short tempered, using the excuse that everybody does it, and blaming others because they have it all. Actually, these feelings, no matter how real they might feel, come from fear. You can see that very clearly. People who behave this way perceive a world full of enemies and arm themselves against it. They usually also have a dislike for employers and government agencies, even though these are almost always the source of their monthly income. Actually, they dislike themselves. In such cases a balance will never be reached in money, power and love, and the battle they experience can go on ad infinitum.

It's important to know that fear always invokes more fear, and that fear of lack and an abundance of money power love cannot go together. This will be reflected at every level, also with friends and lovers.

Learn to receive!

You can learn how to receive. By learning, we don't mean you sit down and memorize a bunch of rules. We mean that you learn to think about the following tips in your daily life and answer the following questions now and then, just for yourself.

- Learn to accept compliments.
- Live in the present.
- What did you receive today, and how did that feel?
- When do you feel burdened when you receive?
- When do you feel guilty?

USING

The flow has three facets. The first is receiving. The second is using. Using is an indispensable aspect. We see a lot of people around us who are unable to enjoy the daily flow of money, power and love. It's also important to know that money, power and love don't just come out of nowhere. All three exist because they love to be used!

We'll assume that you're now totally capable of receiving, that you've totally opened yourself to the wonderful gifts of the universe in the form of money, power and love. How wonderful when every day great quantities of money, power and love come your way! One of the conditions is that you have to use the energy. Just the way electricity becomes light, money transforms itself into food, a house, a donation to a good cause, etc. Power transforms itself into setting up an organization, in a family, or in the realization of a project. Love transforms itself into a delightful feeling of being able to be loving, of being able to spread love and share it with your surroundings.

In fact, on a deeper level using means that the energy becomes part of your inner light. By saying "yes" to the gift that came your way, you are actually saying that you deserve it and that you are worthy to enjoy it. From that moment on, you allow your light to shine fully, without restrictions.

Using is also enjoying

Using goes together with enjoying! With enjoying, we literally mean enjoying without any reservations and thus without being afraid it will run out. Without guilty feelings that your power might put others in your shadow, and without being afraid that as a result you'll become more visible and subject to criticism. Without fear that the flow of love that you are feeling will ever cease. Being able to enjoy every form of the energy without being ashamed.

Without feeling guilty

Guilt and shame are strange concepts. They both give the illusion that we should feel guilty, that we should be ashamed of abundance, no matter what the form. Well guess what? Guilt and shame are both false emotions! It's all about learning to enjoy, without letting these feelings limit you in any way. Simply being grateful to be able to receive money and to use it for anything you might think that you need in your life, without having to ask yourself what anybody else thinks about it. After all, it's wonderful to be empowered in full glory and to be able to enjoy it. It is thus a challenge to do so, without fear of the judgment of others. As for the third form of this energy, love, dare to enjoy so much splendid love within and around you without feeling ashamed. In short, dare to use the one energy, no matter what form it takes. No matter how the energy of money, power and love come your way, if you don't immediately embrace and enjoy it to the fullest, you're doing yourself and the energy an injustice.

By embracing everything that comes your way, you're not shortchanging others. Lack doesn't exist unless you want it to.

There is enough money,

enough power,

and enough love

For everyone! Just by embracing it you are in a position to let others take part in your abundance! So really enjoy everything that comes into your life. Ask yourself a question: How does it feel to buy yourself a present? A bouquet of flowers, for example, or a new coat. For you! A really special, pricey dinner for yourself. A vacation, maybe even a trip to an exotic place that you've been longing to take for years. Now be honest, how does it feel?

Enjoying is going beyond the unease!

Do you recognize a feeling of unease with this, or can you open and honestly say that you feel nothing but happiness? A beautiful bouquet of flowers, a delicious dinner, a long trip: we love to surprise others with lots of love and pleasure, don't we? We feel great if we make the other person happy. Now try to surprise yourself. Give yourself a gift and enjoy it just as much as someone else would. Realize that it is just as much a present: a present from the universe to you! The universe gives you a precious gift and looks gratefully on how you are enjoying it.

Not enjoying is bringing things to a standstill

A very good example might be your savings. People save until it's too late to enjoy. Nobody knows exactly what for, but if somebody asks then we manage to immediately come up with a goal. The most obvious thing to note is that this goal always lays in the future, never in the present. We often save for our pension. We must seem crazy. Saving for something when we're not even sure we will ever be able to use it! People save mostly for an illusion. That doesn't mean that we're advising you to take your pension savings to Las Vegas and gamble them all away or to stop saving entirely. But it is a good idea to check now and then and make sure that things are in proportion. If you find yourself denying yourself things here and now, so you can do things in the future, the balance is surely off.

Live in the here and now

Enjoying means staying in the here and now. If you're sitting in a restaurant with friends and you can only talk about some other restaurant where everything is so delicious and where you want to take everybody next time, you're living in the future. While you're on vacation, planning the next vacation is also clearly aimed at the future.

As soon as something is aimed at the future there is no use, and the flow stops

One of the nicest ways to stimulate abundance is to live in the present. In fact, the present is the only time that exists. That's only logical: yesterday is gone and tomorrow has yet to come! Still, there are more decisions made based on the past or future than you may think. Good things know no time. Love knows no time. Every time you're busy with the past, you stop the flow. Every time you postpone the start of something new and thus move it to the future, you also postpone the stimulation of the flow to the future.

If you receive a good salary and save it all, you avoid stimulating the flow for years. The only possible result is that the flow will eventually stop. If you have difficulty using and thus have difficulty enjoying, you can practice living in the here and now by giving yourself a present now and then. If you find this hard, start small at first and slowly give yourself increasingly bigger presents. You will see that your financial situation, the power in your life and the amount of love you can awaken will grow along with your presents.

PASSING ON

The last facet of the flow is passing it on. This is the third step of the flow cycle. This last step also works just the way we breathe. After inhaling and using all your air, there comes a moment when you have used up all the oxygen and there is nothing left to do but exhale. Likewise, this is the way every form of energy works. Passing it on is the third step in the cycle of flowing. Passing it on seems very easy at first. You go downtown to the shopping center and decide to pass everything on to the clothing stores. Or you go to the furniture store or your favorite car dealer and order everything your heart desires. Finally you have a reason to buy everything that catches your eye! Unfortunately, letting money burn a big hole in your pocket isn't the same thing as passing it on in a spiritual sense. Passing it on is an act of love and a question of making conscious decisions in your life. It's all about what you give, why you are giving it, and who you are giving it to. Throwing energy away is the opposite of spirituality and the opposite of love for yourself and the energy.

Energy is movement

People receive all kinds of things in their lives. The idea is to use them with real gratitude and no guilt. Then comes a time to pass the energy on. That's the only way to keep money, power and love in constant motion. As soon as one of the facets of the flow of receiving, using, and passing on stops, the whole flow stops. Even if you have no problem with the first two facets but have trouble passing the energy on, that in itself is enough to block the flow, no matter how good you are at the first two.

Passing it on is an act of love

You are probably familiar with the story of A Christmas Carol by Charles Dickens. It's a story that's usually performed right before Christmas. It's about a real miser. At the beginning, you see how hardened and lonely the miser really is and how much trouble he has passing things on. The story then goes on to show how he comes in contact with the people around him, and they hold up a mirror to show his true reflection, how far from love he really is. He slowly comes back in contact with the idea of love, his heart opens up, and he is once again able to give. This reestablishes a loving contact with his fellow human beings, and he is far more able to feel the true meaning of abundance. The beauty of A Christmas Carol is that it's a wonderfully illustrative example of money, power and love, because as soon as the miser "thaws out," you see that he not only allows money but also power and love to flow. In the story they also clearly go together.

That's what happens in daily life. Every time you pass it on, your heart opens up a little bit further and you make contact with another part of yourself and others. The part that isn't ruled by fear. It's the part of you that's able to accept others for what they are.

To give is to open yourself

To give is an act of love. That becomes obvious if you realize that by really giving, without reservations, and straight from the heart, you're giving a piece of yourself to someone else. By approaching someone with an open heart, you're actually giving that person a wonderful gift.

Giving isn't the same as suffering

Once we were invited to a concert. Not just any concert, but a concert by someone whose music and outlook on life we admire: Carlos Santana. He's also a major proponent of recognizing and using your own inner power and opportunities in life. The invitation came directly from Santana's office in the USA, and we decided to go. It proved to be a real treat, because the tickets we received were VIP tickets and we were pampered with wonderful things to eat and drink and fantastic seats. We really enjoyed the music, mostly because we saw that the band and Carlos were relaxed and fully focused on stage and were sharing their energy with the audience. Every band member on stage was totally himself! They gave each other space, were really connected, and together they created an atmosphere filled with love. It was an extraordinary performance - one that we've experienced to that extent only with the Santana Band.

The following day, a critic wrote that he hadn't enjoyed the show. The music was good, the band hadn't made any mistakes, but he found that it all went too easy. This clearly shows that the writer has a preference for "the hard way." Carlos Santana and his band actually laid themselves bare, by daring to be on stage exactly who they truly were. Without a façade and without tricks that serve only to strengthen the ego.

That is a clear illustration of "suffering aspect" that's so prevalent in today's society. People think that doing the right thing is the same as suffering and denying themselves all kinds of things. Everything that comes easily and effortlessly isn't a challenge for the ego and is considered superficial. What if life were simply good? Suffering and sweating are nothing but fear of abundance and by definition ego based. If you're truly in the flow, everything goes effortlessly.

Leading and guiding others are the way to pass on money, power and love. Suffering is letting all three forms pine away and is thus the opposite.

Giving is a great gift

Passing the energy on is also an act of joy. Be it to a person, company or government agency, you don't begrudge them. In the section above where we explained about money, we talked about how important it is to pass on everything with love and not just because you have to. There's a reason. If you are unable to pay with pleasure, you're in a state of ungratefulness and will stop the flow. If you pay your bills reluctantly, you're closing off the channel of money, power and love. The same law applies to power and love, as you now know. By closing off the channel of love, you're shortchanging yourself and others and are also able to give less. It's therefore very important to examine your old emotions, those based on fear, set patterns and dogmas, and to quickly let them go, so that you can make the gift of giving larger and larger. Think about the following piece of wisdom:

A gift to the world is a gift to yourself

THE FLOW IS ONE

The three facets - receiving, using and passing on - have been described and explained individually, and all three have their own individual place in life. In that sense they are separate and are not mutually interchangeable. However, many tend to think that the cycle of *receiving, using* and *passing on* is actually a series of successive moments, as if we first need to receive, then use, and eventually pass on. That would also imply that we can receive and use in the present and postpone passing on for the future.

Receiving, using, and passing on is one

The apparent succession of the moments is only an illusion - it doesn't really happen that way. All three facets happen at the same time! They not only belong together, they depend on one another. Only together can the energy truly flow. It's important to remember this when contemplating these ideas. Every movement of energy is complete in and of itself, because the three facets happen at the same time. Thus, you receive, you use (enjoy) and at the same time an exchange takes place.

The energy cycle

The energy cycle is always in balance. You receive, use, and pass it on, you give something. The total amount of energy within a cycle never increases or decreases. It is about staying in the flow the best way possible, so that your channel of money, power and love keeps growing. As a result, you will experience great abundance.

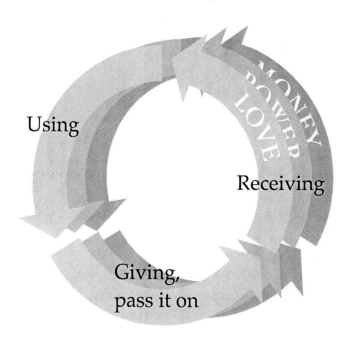

Flowing is the movement of energy

If we receive something, we're not only getting something but at the same time we're also giving

something. The aspects of flowing take place at the same moment. One energy form is thus immediately replaced by another form of the same energy. Because both of these seemingly separate energy flows happen at the same time, you never become poorer! You give something and you immediately receive something in return! Only the form changes.

The universe is an efficient whole

Matter becomes energy; energy becomes matter. One form is converted into another form. The balance changes continually and yet nothing really changes. The universe is a closed system in which not a single particle of energy - not one atom - is ever lost.

For example, you go to a showroom, you buy a car, and you pay a certain amount of money. It's easy to think that you're a certain amount of money poorer and a car richer. But if it was a fair deal, you are no richer or poorer. In essence nothing has changed! Only the outer form of the energy is different. Or imagine you work for somebody. You invest love and power in your work or in a particular company or organization. This investment, this power and love, is usually compensated financially, with money. Also in this case, if the work situation is a good one, you lose nothing when you receive something else in return. Also in this case, nothing has changed! Only the outer form of the energy is different. It's therefore important to realize that you can never become poorer by letting go of money, power, or love! Just the opposite is true. By constantly setting this flow in motion and keeping it in motion, the flow will only grow larger and more powerful.

We see all around us many people who are instinctively afraid to keep this flow moving, because they think that their amount of "energy" will get used up. They have the feeling that the amount will lessen through their purchasing things. That they will become poorer by having to share with others and experience a loss of control and certainty. What they would really love to do is stop the flow altogether and be sure that what they possess now will be there forever.

Wanting to halt the flow is a desire that comes forth out of lack of trust in the future, in yourself, and in the inexhaustible well. It's caused by fear. In fact, fear is a lack of trust, and a lack of trust is nothing but a lack of love for yourself. Otherwise, you would not only know that you deserve the best, but you would also feel it deep within. By deciding to love yourself more, you can help the flow flow more easily. The more you love yourself, the more you trust life, and the more prepared you are to accept the fact that the source of energy is inexhaustible, the greater is your channel of abundance.

What about the state of your "budget" when you've spent a lovely afternoon in your favorite store and bought everything— and we mean everything—that caught your eye and consequently have no money left to do any grocery shopping? Also in that case, you are no poorer than before. You now own a pile of stuff. If that pile of stuff doesn't make you happy enough or means that you're unable to eat, there are two things you can do. You can blame the money, the stores, and your state of "poverty," or you can learn to handle this energy of money, power and love. Even in this case, you received what you paid for. Wasting energy has nothing to do with the belief in abundance; it is purely an attachment to lack and struggle. As you will see later, this is one of the roads to lack.

Energy is inexhaustible

The energy in its purest form is like a babbling brook. A beautiful, lovely stream that flows from one spot to the next. In this case from the great, inexhaustible source to you. In your daily life, you can actually imagine this as being like a stream. As long as no obstacle is put in its way, the water will keep flowing to you. As long as the water flows regularly and in sufficient quantity, the stream will keep getting wider and thus more powerful. Every brook can grow into a river.

Then the human aspects come into play. We become afraid that the water will run out and we build a dam. Finally there's enough, or so we think. A couple of months later it appears that your surrounding land is getting too wet, the plants' roots are losing their strength, and nothing is growing like it should. Another month later and the life in the stream is disappearing. The fish are dying, and the quality of the water is going bad because it doesn't flow anymore. Not much later the fish get so sick they can't be eaten anymore and the water becomes undrinkable. Now we're really in trouble! We try to compensate for the undrinkable water by laying down pipes and we substitute our fresh fish with fish from hatcheries, which isn't the way it was supposed to be. The thing is, we already had all of that. There was good drinking water and there were fresh, healthy fish in abundance. It's because of fear of lack that we decide to dam up the flow, and by doing so we limit ourselves.

The energy is always present in the great universal well in inexhaustible quantities. That has always been so. The only reason we perceive it differently is because we think from the idea of lack. People believe in lack! Thinking from the idea of lack is the only reason why people feel the need to control energy in all its forms. We need only let go of our limits to be able to make use of it fully. There is sufficient energy, we only think otherwise. It's our belief in poverty and struggle that keeps us in our place. It is the denying of this one energy of money, power and love that keeps us in our place.

The world is full of great quantities of money, power and love. There are overwhelming quantities of it present. It's simply about believing that you too are a part of this abundance! There is no lack of love. There is no lack of divine energy. We can even go a step further: there is no lack of God. By believing in a state of lack, you are actually cutting yourself off from abundance. By cutting yourself off from abundance, you are cutting yourself off from God. By telling yourself that you not only deserve abundance but *are abundance*, you're reconnecting with the divine.

There isn't any path to money, power and love. However, there is a path of money, power and love. In fact, there isn't any path to abundance. *You are either in a state of lack or you are in a state of abundance.* The whole gray area in between is an illusion. Every time you say that you want more money, you're confirming to yourself that you're in a state of lack. Every time you say "I need love," you're confirming your lack.

Everything you feel, think, say, and do
is an exchange of energy

Love is present in abundance. There are large quantities of power. And take it from us, money is also present in every needed quantity. There is no such thing as lack. There are only many, many ways to believe that you can cut yourself off from the divine source. Once you get used to the feeling of lack, there are many ways to convince others of your conviction and your fears. Because not only is love contagious, but fear is also contagious and by its nature easily transferable from person to person and from country to country.

Light is a magnet

You can incorporate true abundance into your life by increasing your inner light. Light attracts. Light attracts money, power and love like a magnet. Many people think that increasing one's light is a question of receiving more and more until you have so much money, power and love that you're satisfied. That's not how it works. Others think it's only a question of giving, giving, giving until you finally reach the goal of ultimate enlightenment. That's also incorrect.

The idea is to be able to start cooperating with your surroundings in an honest manner. By cooperating we mean entering into a personal relationship or creating a loving family with your partner, entering into a business agreement, selling something to someone else, or holding an important social position in business or politics. Honest cooperation means that an exchange of energy takes place that fits. If the energy exchange works, there's no need to talk about a giving or receiving party. Both parties are giving and receiving!

Abundance isn't at another's expense

It is most definitely possible to acquire money, power and love without anyone else becoming poorer. In fact, you can acquire true abundance only if you ensure that nothing is gained at cost to another.

If you close a deal in an honest manner,
the other party isn't any poorer

This also becomes apparent in one's work and in the products and services that one provides to another. It's easy to forget that those products and services are actually the same energy as money, power and love. You don't deliver a product, you deliver love! Everybody delivers what and who he is. And that starts with everything that you think. Thus, when you do something for someone else, you have to do it out of love. We don't just mean that you make something with love and then pass it on with love, but also that you are in a state of love when you are making it and passing it on. At that moment, you share your state of being with the person who receives it from you. When you pass something on to another, what you give is an extension of what you are. A job done or a product sold is thus much more than merely what you see, and people really feel this. The moment you realize this and consciously take it into account, a wonderful exchange of energy takes place in which both parties give and both parties receive.

A true exchange of energy means that both parties are richer

If you want more of something, you shouldn't worry about the other person or the product; you need to think about who you are and what you can share. It's about increasing your light. It's a fact that every client, every colleague, and every boss will be more than willing to let energy in the form of money, power, or love flow your way if they can share in your light.

To give is to share

A musician who shares his music with thousands of people in a large stadium isn't selling a product; he's sharing a state of being with many others. It's personal light and the love that is in the music and in the whole performance that is being shared with the public for a couple of hours. That's why people love to hear or see their favorite musician or actor. They share in something that reaches much further than the sounds or images caught on a CD or DVD. They share in pure love. The beauty is, where love flows in such quantities, power and money automatically become visible.

That's the reason why many sports celebrities and actors receive salaries that, according to some, are rather high.

It's only logical! Apparently they are capable of setting in motion so much energy, and thereby allow so much love to flow their way, that power and money also appear in huge quantities in their lives. They set so much energy in motion because they made the decision to share their energy with others. They stand there empowered, do their work with love, and the public pays a certain amount for a ticket. At that moment, both parties are receivers and givers. When that happens there are no longer two separate groups; they share in one energy, a divine energy of love.

Examples such as famous stars like actors, sports celebrities, and musicians not only illustrate the beauty of letting the energy flow in all its forms, but also show the attachment to lack. Not every "star" or sports celebrity is capable of letting go of the attachment to suffering and lack. It's exactly like one of our mothers used to say: "Getting isn't an art; the art is to hold onto it." At the time it was said in connection with love and relationships, but it's a piece of wisdom that also applies to power and money.

As long as you continue to hold on to the feeling of being cut off from the divine source, no matter what the form, at a certain point you'll be confronted with your limitations. You may be able to set large amounts of money, power and love in motion, but you'll tend to lose it just as quickly. If you look closely, you'll recognize this very clearly. Some people can handle this abundance, and their responsibilities and initiatives grow, too.

Others cannot handle this abundance and end up in a whirlpool of divorces, business failures, addictions, and drug rehabilitation centers. Ultimately it's in the way you handle the energy. It's about consciousness.

EXCHANGE OF ENERGY

Many ancient documents refer to the wheel of life. Every culture and every faith expresses this in its own words.

We are born and enter the thrilling world that we call life. As long as we're alive, the wheel turns. Sometimes quickly, sometimes slowly, but it turns until the moment we exhale our last breath.

The amount of material things, power, and love that we experience in our lives is directly coupled to the movement of the wheel of life. As soon as the wheel turns slower, we experience "lack." When the wheel starts to pick up speed, we experience abundance again in our lives—abundance in every area. Many think that they have no influence on the speed at which this wheel turns. But that is not the case. In fact, only YOU can influence the wheel of life. If you lead a life in which you banish every form of amazement, every challenge, you'll stop the flow. If control and the avoidance of change is a steadfast part of your life, you stop the flow.

Investment is movement

These impulses are actually small and large investments in energy. Every investment is an impulse. The wheel keeps turning as long as you regularly give it a mighty push. It's literally a wheel of fortune! This wheel ensures that there is abundance as long as it stays in motion. You are the driving force who, at the right moments, has to give the wheel the impulse it needs so that the flow of money, power and love stays in motion.

By actively investing, you start a powerful flow of energy. By investing, we mean truly putting your energy into something. If you desire a better job or position, you have to work for it, put some energy into it, no matter what the form. At that moment you're investing in yourself and in the company or organization you work for. With that you allow others to share in your energy. By sharing that amount of energy with others and your surroundings, you put energy into motion. As a result, the wheel receives a new impulse to turn!

Denying the exchange of energy

As soon as you think you can avoid investing energy, nothing happens. For example, you wish for a better position or a job that's better suited to you, but your fears come floating to the surface. In that case, you want to further yourself in life but without setting in motion a real exchange of energy. You might want to forget that the flow stands for sharing... When you do that, you are ignoring the law of nature that receiving goes hand in hand with passing on. Or perhaps you forgot that the cycle of receiving, using and passing on has to take place simultaneously. You may want to earn an advanced degree but aren't willing to make any sacrifices financially or in terms of power during your studies. Or you may want a promotion at your job, but you're not willing to work harder than you do now and you definitely don't want to take on any more responsibilities. In such cases we aren't willing to actually give anything. That's taking, not sharing. That's not the way to abundance; it's the fast track to lack. The wheel of life, the wheel of money, power and love, is stimulated by your willingness to share. It is your sincere intention, straight from the heart, to offer your work or study environment something that will start the flow.

Exchanging energy is taking responsibility

Every manner of receiving and passing on brings about a movement in energy—movement from someone else to you, and from you to someone else. You know now that the cycle of receiving, using, and passing on happens simultaneously. Thus, energy that you pass on is immediately replaced by new energy. There is always an exchange of energy. You give something, and something comes back.

If you give something and you say, "I don't want anything in return," you'll often get unease and guilt in return. If you say, "Oh, it was nothing," you're actually saying "What I gave is unimportant, so just give something unimportant in return." If the recipient offers a token of thanks and you refuse to accept, you are pushing energy away. In doing so you prevent the other person from completing the exchange of energy and at the same time make clear that what you gave isn't worth anything. The best thing you can do is to immediately give the other person an opportunity to bring the energy back in balance.

Just imagine that after an examination your doctor says to you, "No thanks, I don't want your money. Your love and gratitude for the rest of your life will be sufficient." How would that make you feel? Of course nobody says it like that literally, but that is what people sometimes mean. When you go to the doctor, it's wonderful to be able to give a suitable exchange of energy that feels good to both parties, so that you're both done with the transaction and with the exchange of energy that took place. After that you're free—free of every form of guilt. Money is the most neutral means of exchange. If you want friendship as payment, be honest about it. "I'll give you this computer, but I'd like your friendship in return." Whenever you receive, use, and pass on you should do so in such a way that both sides, both the giver and the receiver, can move on with their lives without any "energy debt." Be clear and precise in the energy exchange.

It's been our experience that most people are not clear enough when it comes to a correct and proper energy exchange. If you're not consciously open to an energy exchange, you'll suffer from energy loss, and that will lead to a loss of money, a loss of power, and a loss of love. The natural law of flowing gives rise to many misunderstandings. "I do what I do out of love, so I don't need anything in return" (which also means no love, friendship, or appreciation). That may sound very kind and loving, and yet it has nothing to do with love, but more with lack of responsibility.

Every flow cycle, no matter whether it starts with giving, using, or receiving, is a movement of energy. At the moment the movement of money, power, or love takes place, a certain quantity of energy moves from one place to another. It's invisible, but it does happen. You finish the cycle, and the exchange is complete. It's a beautiful thing! This principle of exchange goes back centuries. The Mayans in Mexico understood this principle. Every time they ate an animal or plant, they offered something in return. By doing so, they actually gave something back to the earth. The debt was thus immediately repaid. Every person has to comply with the natural law of flowing. That's why all criminals eventually want to be caught. They take and use, but give nothing back.

The completion of a cycle is the only way

to be able to start a new one

BEYOND YOUR COMFORT ZONE

Every person has a comfort zone, the boundaries within which he or she feels comfortable. In this case, we mean of course a zone that stands for a certain amount of money, power and love. If you have less, you feel unsure and needy; if you have more, you often feel a sense of guilt, or at the least a certain amount of unease. Because we are fearful when we are under our minimum and uneasy when we are over our maximum, we humans have a tendency to want to forever stay within these borders. As long as you stay within this safety zone to avoid discomfort, you will limit the possibilities of money, power and love for yourself.

The unique thing about the principle of the comfort zone is that it inevitably brings important relationships between things to light. Everything that falls outside your zone feels like a lack or feels excessive. As soon as you are once again within your "own" zone, you immediately feel at home. When you go further than your zone, either because of circumstances or through your own choice, you'll feel opposition. If you look at the following illustration of the comfort zone, you'll see a randomly chosen zone with a minimum and maximum between dotted lines. This is just an example, but let's assume that it represents your situation.

The zones between the lines indicate how you will assess yourself and others with respect to money, power and love. If you consider a certain salary to be a minimum, you'll see anyone who earns less as "poorer." If that minimum of power is your minimum, you'll judge everybody with less power as "not powerful." If the dotted line indicates the minimal quantity of love you would like to see returned in a relationship, you'll judge every other relationship that looks different on the basis of that norm. The same holds true for everything that goes over the maximum, since that's the maximum amount of energy you can handle. This means that you'll start to feel uncomfortable if you have more or receive more than the maximum that you accept as normal, no matter whether we're talking about money, power, or love. Of course you can ignore this, but it literally means that you cannot handle any more energy.

For instance, if your business becomes successful and grows until it's annual profit is five times what you expected and can handle, you will find yourself in a situation in which you're happy on the one hand but uneasy on the other. The energy for which you are responsible has become greater than your comfort zone. You'll subconsciously do everything in your power to get rid of it or in any case enjoy it as little as possible.

If the maximum of your comfort zone is not very high, you'll see that reflected in all three appearances of the energy. We just talked about money. With power this becomes apparent in your work; if your comfort zone isn't all that high, you'll regularly have a job that you like, but it will eventually lead to conflict, be it with colleagues or your boss. You'll have trouble finding a job where you're happy and stay happy, have wonderful colleagues, and get paid a top salary for your field. A great job with wonderful colleagues and a top salary would be too much for you, because it would be outside your comfort zone. If you handle money and power this way you'll enjoy your work less and less, and if things really take a downturn you might even become depressed.

In your private life this will manifest itself as having enough but never really having superabundance. It will take a lot of work to "get enough." The aspect of power will also be insufficient for you. You'll eventually get lost in mediocrity and lose all your dreams or ambitions. At first glance the aspect of love will seem "reasonable," but if you take a closer look you'll see that the partners take each other for granted and are not really fulfilling each other's deeper needs and desires.

Others will also judge you according to your own comfort zone. Your zone stands for a certain degree of education and dreams for the future. Everything that falls short is "dumb," and everything that rises above is excessive and has attitude. Everything within your zone feels "normal."

Fearfully holding on to the comfort zone that you were "given" limits you immensely. It might be the cause of your feeling inferior around people who have a higher education than you do, or your annoyance with very wealthy people. Or it may be why you often think of starting your own business but never get around to it.

The comfort zone also determines how you feel about society as a whole, including politics, the town council, and taxes. The smaller the zone, the more mistrust toward government agencies, as if they were all scheming against you.

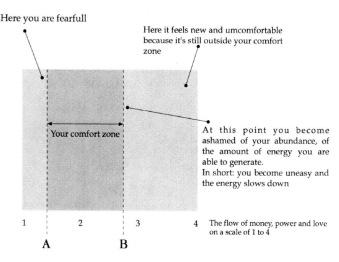

Here you are fearfull

Here it feels new and umcomfortable because it's still outside your comfort zone

Your comfort zone

At this point you become ashamed of your abundance, of the amount of energy you are able to generate.
In short: you become uneasy and the energy slows down

1   2   3   4   The flow of money, power and love on a scale of 1 to 4

A   B

A is the minimum you can handle
B is the maximum you can handle

Test yourself

The "old" way of thinking is that your comfort zone will adjust to the amount of energy that you have available, no matter what the form. However, the natural laws of money power love work the other way around. In time, the "amount" of energy will become equal to your comfort zone. The following exercise is meant to give you the opportunity to "feel" where your comfort zone begins and where it ends. Read the following descriptions and at the same time be aware of what's happening in your body and in your mind. Do you experience tension, blame, joy, or does it seem excessive to you?

Imagine yourself eating out a few times. The first time you go to a small, simple establishment.

The second time you choose a restaurant that's a bit less modest. Then you go to a mid-class restaurant, and after that you go to a classy place, and then to an even more luxurious restaurant. Finally, you top it off with a real five star restaurant, very exclusive, where you're served a five-course meal with the finest wines in beautiful coolers, left and right immaculately dressed waiters serving all kinds of delicacies. You're being waited on like a king. So you start very simple and work your way up, step-by-step, to the most luxurious restaurant you can imagine.

At which moments did you feel uncomfortable, and when were you completely at ease? A feeling of discomfort clearly indicates that somewhere you ran into the borders of your comfort zone, while a feeling of being totally in your element was completely within your comfort zone. If you labeled one of these outings as "unusual" or as "unattainable," then it clearly fell outside your comfort zone.

It's a challenge to expand your comfort zone. Ensure that you feel comfortable and at home in a luxurious restaurant, an exclusive clothing store, or in a gorgeous five-star hotel. Not because they are better than the rest —a small eating establishment and a cozy family run hotel can be just as wonderful as their more luxurious counterparts. It's all about being able to feel at home in the more luxurious places as well. That you know- and above all feel - that this abundance can also be a part of you, without you're feeling uncomfortable. In fact, that's when you feel in your heart that there is no difference between you and all the other people! There's also a king hiding in you. Expanding your comfort zone is important because it allows you to integrate all aspects of society into your existence. Make the other world, that instinctively seems so far away, also your own. Get used to the fact that the world is part of you and you are part of that world.The comfort zone is the secret behind the saying "the world is yours."

The world that you experience is as large as you want it to be

WE ALL ARE ONE

It's funny, people live in a particular country, tend to look a lot like each other, share many values, get married and divorced, and share the same energy in the three aspects of money, power and love. Still, we like to think in terms of *them and us*. We use these words to indicate that we have something that the others don't. Or to indicate that they have a lot and we don't. Or that they are different from what we are. But these terms exist only within the boundaries of our earthly separation mentality and remind us time and again how separated we feel.

The feeling of separation goes hand in hand with the separation from the divine flow of money, power and love. As soon as we "hook up" to the flow of money, power and love, we start a relationship with the All, with the divine in ourselves and thereby with the divine in every other person. As soon as we connect ourselves to that feeling, the realization that we are all one and that every person is in essence love, we bring about a very strong connection with the flow of money, power and love.

Because we all are one, obviously giving really comes down to sharing. You always share with the whole, and by doing so you share with yourself. Giving and taking doesn't apply to others or to yourself. You share. In fact, you share with everything around you and within yourself. You share with God. And God, or the divine if you prefer, is in you, is in the other person, is in everybody. Feeling connected with everything and everyone around you is therefore a very powerful path of abundance.

In our daily lives, it's sometimes difficult to feel this bond all the time. In fact, it's at times when we're confronted with lack, in whatever form it may take, that we can easily feel embittered, and we readily project that feeling onto others, as if others caused our lack. This way of thinking is sometimes even referred to as "thinking from lack." At such times, it's the lack we're experiencing that's in the foreground, rather than our connection with others.

Experiencing and truly feeling, on a daily basis, that we all are one enables you to experience the world more from a feeling of oneness, peace, and above all connectedness. It is this link that binds us not only to others but also to the energy of money, power and love.

Recognize the light in everyone

It follows that we're talking about the ability to recognize the light in others. Of course, some have gotten far removed from their natural state of being, from love and compassion. Still, that doesn't make them any less human. They are human beings, just like you. They also have love to give, they also need love, and are in search of the driving force behind money, power and love. Some people just don't know how to do that very well. They search and search and have lost the way. You can't blame somebody because they're still searching. After all, we all have been searching, only in different ways or at different times. In the end, the driving force behind their search has the same origin as yours. It's a challenge to keep seeing the light that forever shines within, particularly at the most difficult times, and to appeal to that part of others.

PART IV

THE THIRD LAW OF NATURE: ENERGY FOLLOWS THOUGHT

The first law of nature is that money power love is one energy. The second law of nature is that it has to flow. The third law of nature is that energy follows thought. That, in itself, is amazing. It enables the mind to bring about anything we want. Mind you, anything we want, not what we think we want. You see, the mind is able to create two things: lack and abundance. If you think in terms of lack and poverty, the energy will follow. If you start from a state of abundance, the energy will follow.

Because people are programmed by their surroundings, through opinions, words, judgments and unspoken convictions, it's important for people to get a better understanding of the concept of "mind."

People often let themselves be led by roads that lead to lack, even though they might think otherwise. We will therefore discuss the roads that lead to lack in some detail. Fortunately, there are also roads of abundance. These roads are the means to be able to see the natural state of abundance again, to feel it and to activate it in our lives.

Actually, it's a question of how you've managed to keep yourself in a state of lack up to now. Because that is what in fact has happened. There is abundance all around us.

There is no lack of love. Power is already in us, and money is also a birthright just like oxygen and love. We are all in a state of divine abundance, but we maintain the separation between abundance and ourselves. Although it is important to discover which roads to poverty we have traveled up to now, it's not wise to occupy ourselves too much with the roads of lack. By doing so, you are feeding energy to a state of lack, and what you focus on grows. It keeps getting more and more important, becoming larger and larger, until one day it becomes so immense in your life that you can't see the forest for the trees anymore—the only thing you see are the roads to lack. It's like a mountain covered with roads and possibilities that so tempt you that you forget that you were the one that created the mountain in the first place. And that is definitely not what you want.

Still, for many it doesn't feel that way. "I'm not looking for the roads to poverty. I've always been in search of the roads to abundance, the roads to love and oneness." This is precisely what we're talking about. By believing in the "roads to abundance" you're actually walking the road to lack. There aren't any roads to abundance!

Your thoughts, your words, and your vision of the future now stand in the light of lack or the light of abundance. There's nothing in between. What are you really telling yourself when you're consciously looking for the roads to abundance? First, you're telling yourself that you apparently have to do something, that you need to undertake something, in order to acquire abundance, while in fact it's already part of you. Second, you're programming yourself, time and again, that you apparently don't have it. If we take a moment and remember that *whatever we focus on grows*, you begin to understand that this isn't so much a path to abundance as the path to lack. *It's like being in a relationship and at the same time constantly saying "I'm looking for a relationship."*

Fortunately, there's another way: the road of abundance. The road of abundance doesn't lead anywhere. This road is already founded in abundance. Today, tomorrow and in the future.

THE ROADS OF LACK

Wandering the roads to lack isn't very stimulating... To change this, it's necessary to know what these roads are and to catch yourself every time you find yourself walking down one of them.

As you now know, others instinctively know how you think about money, power and love. People also sense whether you're still traveling down the roads of lack, and they respond to that. Most people don't wander down all the roads that lead to lack; they follow only a few of them. It isn't necessary to walk all of them to avoid a state of abundance - only a few are enough. And as soon as your life is focused on lack and negativity, you'll attract others who are enamored with the same thing. That's when you find yourself stuck in a vicious circle of lack. The trick is not to let it get that far. It's so wonderfully stimulating, also for others, if you dare to distance yourself from the roads of lack and thereby give others the freedom to do the same!

The ways to lack are described below. The sequence in which they're given here doesn't say anything about their relative importance.

Before you go on with the paths of lack we would advise you to answer the following questions first.

Continue reading after having completed this exercise!

ABOUT THE QUESTIONS

The following questions represent the pitfalls in life. All 15 are based on everyday life and – if you only look closely enough – you meet these situations nearly every day.

The idea is to answer each question in all honesty. So please, don´t write down what might be considered politically correct or what sounds good or really spiritual... You´re doing this for yourself!

Start by reading each question aloud once or twice to yourself and then answer it.

Example

Take the first question: Do people sometimes find you cynical? Maybe you don´t look upon yourself as a cynic but deep inside you know very well that occasionally you can be or you know that that´s what others think of you – in that case, this attitude is somehow part of you and so the answer must be yes.

Variation

Once you finished the exercise, you could answer every question three times:

How you used to think about it, how you think about it right now and how you would like to see it in the future.

THE QUESTIONS

1. Do people sometimes find you cynical?

2. Do you sometimes think others possess a lot, undeservedly?

3. Do you think that there are moments in which you are the plaything of circumstances?

4. Do you feel sorry for other people now and again?

5. Do you believe in a supernatural/divine power?

6. Can you see money, power and love as one and the same force?

7. Do you sometimes have disorder in your life?

8. Do you keep things, although you haven't used them for a long time?

9. Are you late more often than twice per year?

10. Do you consider yourself to be a courageous and dynamic person?

11. Do you feel someone is entitled to support from society?

12. Taking From The Rich To Give To The Poor?

13. Do you often look for special offers or bargains?

14. Does a relationship appeal to you where partners are attracted and rejected in turns?

15. Are you in search of spirituality and/or abundance?

ANSWERS AND CLARIFICATION

1) Cynicism

Question: Do people sometimes find you cynical?
Ideal answer: No
Deeper meaning: Rejection of energy.

By cynicism we mean the ability to look at and judge everything that happens in the world or in one's immediate surroundings with sarcasm and ridicule. The true cynic considers himself very sensible and objective and therefore considers himself very qualified to judge in matters of politics, art, and culture. It's the curse of the cynic that he rejects every form of wonderment and joy, just to be able to keep his authoritative position. It's this armor of unfeeling carelessness with which he tries to lift himself above life so as not to have to take part in it. It's this armor that gives the cynic a feeling of safety, because it stands between the person himself and the energy of money power love. It's this armor that ensures that the two cannot make any contact at all.

2) Being against Possessions

Question: Do you sometimes think others possess a lot, undeservedly?
Ideal answer: No
Deeper meaning: Begrudging others their energy.

Someone who's against possessions doesn't think he's against possessions, only against excessive possessions. He thinks possessions are fine, as long as they are divided up fairly. The person who's against possessions doesn't realize that by being so conditional, he's rejecting every form of possession and has therefore lost contact with the energy. By stubbornly refusing to look with joy at the wonderful abundance of others and to be truly happy for them, such persons are placing themselves on the side of the "anti-possessors."

3) Feeling Sorry for Yourself

Question: Do you think that there are moments in which you are the plaything of circumstances?
Ideal answer: No
Deeper meaning: Wanting to attract energy by means of lack.

Feeling sorry for yourself, or seeing yourself as the victim of all kinds of circumstances that you can't do anything about, is an excellent way to stop the flow. The flow of money, power and love is there for everybody, regardless of your social class or education, unless you feel sorry for yourself or see yourself as a victim. You can feel sorry for yourself in many different ways. Perhaps you feel sorry for yourself because you don't have a partner at the moment, or because you're a single parent blessed with four kids who are still in school and who need a lot of care. Or maybe you've been suffering from some physical ailment that keeps you from being as carefree as you used to be. You think at the very least you're a bit pathetic. Or perhaps you aren't feeling sorry for yourself but consider yourself a victim of circumstances. That's often how it feels. You have a wonderful family, a couple of kids, a fine house, and then your partner decides to leave you. So there you are. A life in ruins. In truth a phrase like "a victim of circumstance" doesn't exist. The last two words can be left off. If you feel like a victim of circumstance, you're just a victim. The "me-again" syndrome also belongs in this category. "Me again" is a confirmation, time and time again, of being a victim and not being able to do anything about it. And a victim is without question no longer in the flow—at the most they're in someone else's flow. The more you pity yourself, the stronger the bond with your unpleasant situation becomes. The challenge is to transform these feelings when you find yourself in a situation in which you have every reason to feel sorry for yourself. Not for others, but for yourself.

4) Feeling Sorry for Others

Question: Do you feel sorry for other people now and again?
Ideal answer: No
Deeper meaning: Expanding your energy at the cost of another.

You can feel sorry for others from close by or from far away. One person may obtain his information from newspapers and television, while another experiences the world from close up, in his own environment. You can hear and read about everything these days. Wars, poverty, disease, persecutions, refugees, and famine. The list is long and becomes longer as each year passes. That's strange, because the West is much more concerned with this misery than it used to be, thanks in part to modern media such as television and the Internet. Why is it that things keep getting worse instead of better? It's because we feel so "sorry" for them. When you feel sorry for someone else, you're loading their misery on your own shoulders, and from that moment on that's what you're spreading. Feeling sorry for others puts them in the role of victim and makes the gap between their world and ours that much larger. The misery they're going through doesn't make them lesser people. They're still people just like anyone else, with real feelings and real opinions. By feeling sorry for them we are placing them in the category of victims, while as a people or as a country they're trying to shed that image.

However, there's nothing wrong with wanting to do something about it. Not because they're pitiful, but just because they're fellow human beings. Just like you give your son an allowance because he needs it and you're happy to do it, you can also help others the same way. You don't have to feel sorry for your kids before you support them! In the same way, it's fine and useful to share with others. With the same love and the same intentions. To stop pitying people is not only better for your own flow; it's also much better for theirs. As long as you're feeling sorry for others, you aren't really able to do anything about their situation. Feeling sorry paralyzes the giver of the pity, as well as the receiver. As soon as you stop nourishing this feeling, you're in a position to really help in a manner that can be useful—active, useful and effective, without enervating others.

5) Not Believing in a Higher Power

Question: Do you believe in a supernatural/divine power?
Ideal answer: Yes
Deeper meaning: Keeping yourself apart from the energy and from others.

If you cannot or will not believe that there is something that connects us, an inner, loving power, a divine consciousness, God, anything divine, you've delivered yourself to the wolves. We don't mean believing in a punishing God or an all-powerful and oppressing God, but the God of wisdom, of love, of compassion and solidarity. A power that's not above us but present within all of us. You can call it whatever you like: God, Divinity, the Higher Power, Christ Consciousness, Allah, Buddha, Energy, Inner Power, Prana or Love. Denying this power is the same as rejecting the energy of money, power and love, which will lead to conflict in both your inner world and outer world. As a result, life becomes tiring and lonely. This ultimately leads to embitterment.

6) Denying that Money, Power and Love is One Energy

Question: Can you see money, power and love as one and the same force?
Ideal answer: Yes
Deeper meaning:
Believing in an energy full of struggle and difficulties.

Acknowledge that money, power and love is one energy. They all originate from the same place. All three fulfill the same laws of nature. As long as you don't really feel this, or even worse deny it, you'll stop the natural flow and end up in a way of life in which cynicism, lack, manipulation, and struggle will be your only friends. Acknowledging that everything is one and that everything influences everything else brings love back in your life and puts you back in touch with other people, with yourself, and with the energy we all have within us.

7) Disorder

Question: Do you sometimes have disorder in your life?
Ideal answer: No
Deeper meaning:
Affirming to yourself that there is a "lack" of the energy.

Disorder is a clear and recognizable way to bring a state of lack into your life. We mean disorder, clutter and chaos. Disorder in the way you think, in your house, your finances, your planning, your relationships—you'll find it on many levels. For instance, clutter in your home. Things are everywhere, your papers spread out here and there, books next to your bed or under the table. In short, a mess. Of course you don't have to be a clean freak, but not being able to quickly find your belongings means you don't have your affairs in order. In fact, that's what it's all about, having your things and thus your life in order. Your home or your room is a mess; you don't really know what you want to study, or you know but change your mind every six months. If your life is not entirely in order, you don't know what you want, your relationship doesn't fare smoothly, you have arguments with your parents or your ex, then your house keeps getting messier and you don't feel like cleaning it up. The energy is missing. That's exactly what it's all about: the energy is missing. The nice thing about this is that it's very easy to change this situation. Cleaning up and bringing order in your life isn't all that hard. But if it feels that way, and you can't even work up the energy, then you have your answer even before you ask the question.

8) *Saving and Holding on to Everything*

Question: Do you keep things although you haven't used them for a long time?
Ideal answer: No
Deeper meaning:
Hoarding energy.

Some people have a hard time getting rid of anything. For some, picking something up, putting it in a garbage bag, and throwing it away is a painful experience. They think about sorting things out and throwing things away, they may talk about it, but there's always an excuse to hold on to some of it or put it in a box, "where it wont be in anybody's way," for safe keeping. Saving or holding on to things causes the flow of money, power and love to stop. Of course, saving and holding on are relative terms; what's really old and useless and what isn't? Everything that you haven't used for three years can go. Clothes, junk, your old bike, furniture, everything. Do you have boxes with books that you never look at, that you don't need for your work, and you don't have a professional library? Get rid of them!

If you're still holding on to things, it's an indication that you want to stop the natural process of change. In that case, you don't really want another job, another house, and often even another, real relationship. This phenomenon often occurs in phases. Money, power and love require a life in motion, and this motion returns at every level, also in the matter around you. Collecting goes much further than *collecting things*. It's actually about a quantity of memories, about a "frozen" quantity of energy filled with the past and emotions, but without a future. The more material objects with a past you collect, the less abundance.

9) Being Late

Question: Are you late more often than twice per year?
Ideal answer: No
Deeper meaning:
Not being able to handle the flow of energy.

There's always a reason. It was Labor Day. Your son was sick. A bad cold. You couldn't find a cab. The trains were running late. Your partner unexpectedly couldn't bring you. Your neighbor's house was on fire. They're the kinds of excuses that come into your life if you're uncomfortable in the flow. From our experience, people who often come late and sometimes don't show up at all are having problems with the energy of money, power and love. If you don't have that "problem" yet, you only have to stop keeping your appointments and start turning up late regularly and a state of lack will arise by itself. In society there are also codes of conduct that are linked to this. At some companies, if you show up late for a job interview you can just as well not bother to come at all.

If you're regularly late, you're placing yourself outside the flow of money, power and love. You're actually afraid to claim your place in a normal and powerful manner.

Some savvy companies ask clients in advance how much time they have to complete an assignment. They want to know if the assignment is a rush job before making the decision to give the client (usually a new one) a line of credit. If a new client is disorganized, plans poorly, and is always late, that client will probably also be unreliable about paying your invoices. We've intentionally mentioned a new client, because that kind of client will never be satisfied and thus will always be hopping from one company to another.

10) Lack of Courage and Dynamism

Question: Do you consider yourself to be a courageous and dynamic person?
Ideal answer: Yes
Deeper meaning:
Not daring to set the wheel of energy in motion.

If you don't dare take the step of being courageous in life —having the courage to undertake things, to get out of your easy chair, to take risk, to take initiative, to take a position—the flow of money, power and love will stop. We're not talking about heroism, that's not necessary, but about plain courage, about pluck, about a certain dynamism in your behavior, your attitude, and your decisions. The courage to take a stand in life instead of staying quietly in the background being moved along by the courage of others. Every time that you gather your courage and do something, regardless of the consequences, you set something beautiful in motion. Your courage and dedication set a massive amount of energy into motion, and that's what it's all about! Love, energy in motion. You'll recognize a lack of courage by a heavy dose of hesitation, a wait-and-see attitude, and a certain kind of laziness. Not only physical laziness, but also mental laziness.

11) "You Take Care of Me"

Question: Do you feel someone is entitled to support from society?
Ideal answer: No
Deeper meaning:
Wanting to live of the energy of others.

Actually, the opposite of courage is the thought "you take care of me." The 'you' in this case could be the welfare office, the insurance agency, or your neighbors, friends, and family. If the idea of feeling victimized is nourished long enough, the ultimate state of being pitied and victimized is reached: "You take care of me." Not because you're a fellow human being or because they really want to, but because you make them feel like you're entitled to it. You are entitled to their help. If people don't give you the help you expect immediately and in the form you expect, you let them know right away—by making them feel guilty—that they apparently can't be bothered with you. As human beings we tend to think we're open to life, to abundance, by being open to receiving aid. And that is partly true. However, that's something completely different from taking it for granted that others will take care of you. That's the ultimate way to enervate yourself and actually tell the outside world that you aren't capable of awakening the energy of money, power and love. Eventually that will become your reality, which will strengthen your dependence on others and ultimately your belief that you can't do it on your own!

12) The "Robin Hood Effect"

Question: Taking From The Rich To Give To The Poor?
Ideal answer: No
Deeper meaning: Taking energy from others without permission.

In the extension of the "you take care of me" attitude lies the Robin Hood effect. You're now able to plunder without feeling guilty. How wonderful! You think that you don't have to pay the doctor's bill because he has plenty of money anyway. As if he would even notice! You don't even feel consciously guilty when you walk out of the supermarket with a couple of glossy magazines under your arm—the supermarket won't miss them! This is sometimes even referred to as proletarian shopping. As soon as you integrate into your life the idea that you can just take from the rich, you completely stop the flow of money, power and love. Suddenly everything revolves around you, and the concept of sharing from your side has been lost entirely. The flow of money, power and love is optimal if every transaction is honest and the exchange of energy is voluntary and mutual.

13) Believing in Bargains

Question: Do you often look for special offers or bargains?
Ideal answer: No
Deeper meaning:
Fear of really sharing the energy.

This is one of the most difficult principles to really understand and recognize. There's no such thing as a bargain. You get what you pay for. Because that's precisely the amount of energy you're willing to set in motion. Still, it often feels different. Every time we read about fabulous offers in the newspaper or when we walk around at the supermarket, we always hope that something like a bargain really exists. The best Bordeaux for the price of a table wine. Once you start incorporating this knowledge, you'll find that this learning comes in phases. At first you recognize that it really is true for material things like homes, cars, wines, and clothing. Quality has its price. Later, you discover that it also holds true for power. One training course is not the same as another; a good course that you will benefit from and really get something out of has a price. You might think love is the exception. Love comes from above and knows no price. Well guess what? There are no bargains in love either. If you truly want love in your life, you'll discover that it also involves investing. Investing in yourself and in your surroundings. And investing is sharing. The flow of money, power and love knows no exceptions and knows no bargains!

14) Romanticizing Suffering

Question: Does a relationship appeal to you where partners are attracted and rejected in turns?
Ideal answer: No
Deeper meaning:
Not at ease when receiving energy in abundance. You took refuge in 'repel and attract' so it's never completely yours...

A well-traveled path of lack is the romanticizing of suffering and the belief in "difficulty." We read novels about impossible love, relationships where the partners hurt one another, and children born out of loveless marriages or short, passionate romances. Unfortunately, this is not restricted to such popular books. Many people thrive on human suffering. Relationships in which we hurt one another, confirming each other's incapacity to really love, arguments, infidelity, nothing is left unexploited. People seem to be enslaved to conflict and difficulty. A relationship that runs smoothly and awakens what is most beautiful in a man and in a woman, is often labeled as boring. The tension, the hurting, the mock battle of hate and love, that's what it's all about! Then we feel alive again! That is why many of us love watching television. One person watches a "romantic" series, in which the fog, the drink, and unreachable love remind us that life can be hell. Another watches a soap that teaches that ultimate pleasure consists of shallow relationships and cheating on each other. We enjoy the pain; we romanticize the suffering. It is this attachment to suffering that separates us from love, and thereby from the flow of money, power and love. There is such a thing as relationships between people that do not thrive on the negative energy of hate and love, that need no strife and mistrust. That's how you awaken the energy of love and trust in each other, so that you can face the world together, as a team. If something feels too easy, many have a tendency to feel guilty. If it's difficult, people think they really deserved it. The necessity of strife and difficulty is an illusion!

15) Always Searching

Question: Are you in search of spirituality and/or abundance?
Ideal answer: No
Deeper meaning: Wanting to force the energy.

Being in search of love, of power, or of material things are all the same. It's about being in search of the one energy. As long as you're searching for ways to receive a particular form of abundance—as long as you're trying to find ways to get more money or talk about being more powerful—you're walking the path of lack. Searching, wanting, thinking, and often even talking about it, stops you from one thing: doing. It's not possible to "find" love somewhere. You are love at that moment or you're not. Power isn't for sale; you're either in a state of power or you're not. Money can't be "found"; you're in a state of abundance or you're not. Every moment of the day, you have a new choice.

With abundance it's not about the amount or the struggle to obtain it; it's about whether or not you can feel abundance deep in your heart. If you discover in yourself that you have the tendency to go looking for money, power, or love, it's important to stop doing so immediately. People then often ask how it's possible to create a nice life for yourself and your surroundings without chasing and searching. The answer is that to acknowledge a desire that you have is a very good thing, but to search for fulfillment is disastrous. Change is a decision.

Life is like a feather. The harder you run after a feather, the more commotion you make, the faster it will fly away from you. But you can decide to do it differently. You move slowly toward the feather, relaxed and trusting.

You casually hold out your hand, and the feather nestles itself in your palm.

"There is no road to success...

Success is the road"

Buddha

COMPLETE SUMMARY

Now have a look and check if your answers coincide with the desired answers and if not, note the different answers down and count them.

More than 10 paths of lack:
We would advise you to have a close look at the question why you seem to cling so much to the paths of lack. This is not caused by the paths themselves but just by your own clinging to them.

Less than 10, more than 5:
You're heading in the right direction but seem to still cling to a number of paths of lack. Ask yourself the following question:

Which part of me still clings to ..... ?
(..... is the path of lack concerned)

Less than 5 paths of lack:
You're really heading the right way and are walking well on the path of abundance. Your clinging to the paths of lack has diminished by almost two thirds! Now your courage for the last bit is required... Be aware that in times of stress or heavy mental strain old patterns and barriers may appear again. That gives you the chance to grow even more.

THE ROADS OF ABUNDANCE

Once again, it's important to realize that there are no roads to abundance: you either walk the path of abundance or you don't! To say "the path to" suggests you are on your way to something; simply "walking a path" means that you are already walking it NOW.

The roads described here acknowledge the natural situation of abundance in which we human beings already find ourselves. They ensure that you are able to leave behind the ways in which you limited yourself before. The subjects that follow are all equally valuable. They aren't listed in any particular order.

1. CREATING THOUGHTS

There are very few people who have never heard of the power of positive thinking. Why is positive thinking so important? Positive thinking means the end of negative thinking, and that means that you stop walking the road of lack.

Through positive thinking, you're actually saying, "I don't see any reason to view everything in a negative light, because I know I deserve abundance." That's why it's so important to think positive! Everything that you think has an enormous effect on the flow of money, power and love. If you say, "I don't know if I can do it," all power instantly flows out of you and the flow stops. On the other hand, if you say, "I can do it," your attitude holds a promise in itself. In that case there is power, there is love, and there is money. It is precisely this attitude that starts the flow and wil keep it moving. At that moment you have something you can share with others! The effect of positive thinking reaches much further than the mind itself. It also influences your state of being as a whole and even your physical body, including your overall health and your immune system. At the moment you utter the sentence, "I don't know if I can do it," your power literally flows out of your body. You actually become physically weaker! If you say the sentence, "I can do it," you become mentally and physically stronger. You also become more resistant to illness, stress, and everything that might undermine your physical and mental constitution.

Positive thinking is sometimes misunderstood, as if you could get what you want just by saying often enough that you want it. That is not entirely correct. In fact, the more you say, "I want happiness" or "I'm searching for happiness," the less chance you have of ever being happy, because the idea "I want" is the most powerful way possible to convince the cosmos that you don't have it. The same applies to ideas like "I hope," "I think that," "I wish," "I want," and everything else that's aimed at the future and that isn't taking place in the here and now. So the more words you use that carry the underlying connotation that you don't have it now, the "worse" you make things. Even if you are just beginning the process of recognizing the abundance of money, power and love, by starting to think positively, you acknowledge that there is abundance. Positive thinking expresses itself in sentences like, "I'm happy, "I feel love," and "I have abundance." Of course it might seem strange to say you have it even though you feel totally different at that moment. It might even feel hurtful and painful. Saying, preferably out loud, that you are happy while on the inside you only feel loneliness and heartache can feel very strange and unreal. But that's what it's all about. The moment you do it, something happens in the deepest part of your being, in every cell in your body, all at once. As a result, you are open to receive the abundance of love, power, and material things. To make perfectly clear what you are actually saying, you could add to every wish you send into the cosmos, "the cosmos will take care of it."

Exercise:

The following exercise will give you more insight. It's very important to know, if a way of thinking will lead to a state of lack, or to a state of abundance. Write your sentence down like 'I want love' or 'I am looking for spirituality' etc.

Then change the sentence in this way:
The cosmos will ensure that you will continue to
.... as long as you live.

Fill in the first blank with the verb you used, like want, wish for, search for, hope for, have, be, feel, etc.
Fill in the second blank with what you wanted in your sentence. If your sentence was "I want happiness" what you get is: The cosmos will ensure that you will continue to want happiness as long as you live.

Kind of a strange sentence, but it clearly shows that this is not what you are looking for! It inevitably leads to wanting forever. That you can continue until the end of your days without ever having achieved it.

If you had the sentence "I am happy," you'll get:

The cosmos will ensure that you will continue to be happy as long as you live.

This sentence clearly shows that you are gladly in a state of happiness. Just being wonderfully happy, without forever wanting to be. Every form of work or hope or dream in which the fulfillment lies in the future, ensures that you will not get it. By work or dreams we mean verbs like wanting, hoping, wishing, and searching. So remember: words that characterize the here and now, like have and be, create abundance.

2. ATTENTION CULTIVATES GROWTH

Everything you pay attention to grows. "Everything we give attention to" deserves closer examination, especially because the explanation and interpretation of the word "attention" is important.

We often think about things that we find important. Sometimes we reaffirm our wishes the whole day. Talking about these kinds of things is also a favorite pastime, especially at parties, get-togethers, and in bars. This is not the attention we mean. You can keep thinking about something for years, even talk about it all day, without ever making it come about! "Attention" goes much farther than thinking and talking about something.

Real attention is the moving of energy from one point to another, from you to what you find important.

The energy of attention is identical to the energy we're talking about, the energy of money, power and love. Giving something attention, letting something grow, is like giving water to a plant. Thinking about the plant and talking about it at length won't help it. It won't grow an inch. Only real action, giving nourishment, makes the plant grow. So it is in life. We tend to take what we treasure, what we think can be used up, like money, power and love, and we want to save it. Why? "Well, you never know." Just imagine, what if your great idea is all-wrong? What if she's not your true love after all? What if putting all your power and energy into that project was a bad idea? What if your business idea flops and you lose all that money? What if ... ?

As long as you're worried about things that might happen ("What if?") and as a result you don't just go for it and keep hedging you bets, the energy flow will stall until you make a decision. You're only giving energy to your doubts instead of to the success of your ideas. If you truly and unconditionally believe in something or someone, it's important to go for it one hundred percent. Without reservations and without wanting to play it safe. That means you have to put money, power and love into it. Everything that you put energy into will grow!

"Everything you pay attention to grows" is one of the most powerful roads of abundance. It gives you the chance to choose anew each day and to give what you find important a powerful boost. When applying this natural law, it's important to remember that it is about all three forms of the energy, not just one or two of them. It's all about the balance. Balance in the underlying relationship of money, power and love, but also balance in the relationship between what you expect out of a project, the amount of energy you put into it, and what you could have invested.

3. Be True to Your Highest Ideals

In everything that you do, it's necessary to be true to your highest ideals, to be true to what you feel is of the utmost importance for you to do in this life. Your highest ideals aren't necessarily the same as doing what you want. "Do whatever feels good and don't do anything that doesn't feel right"; however spiritual that may sound, it often boils down to sidestepping your own blockades, avoiding confrontations with yourself and with others, and fulfilling your own expectations and those of your surroundings.

Staying true to your highest ideals means taking on the challenge of fulfilling the life's goal of your spirit, of your soul. Why are you on earth? What's your assignment here? Why did your soul choose to be here, and what experience does it still need? That is the highest ideal of your soul.

It is useful to regularly take a moment of rest in your life. Rest is more than a short pause between two cups of tea. It's using meditation, or for example a Reiki treatment, to allow yourself to look within and ask yourself what your highest ideal is.

- Is the life I'm leading my highest ideal?

- Is the work I do now my highest ideal?
- Is the relationship I'm in now my highest ideal?
- Is the environment that I've chosen my highest ideal?

The answers to these questions will make it easier to stay true to your highest ideal and thereby walk the path of abundance.

4. RESPECT

We have now covered three roads of abundance. Respect is the last road of abundance, and it holds a special place within money power love because it brings you two things:

- Living from respect changes your energy field, your outlook on life, in such a way that you'll be able to recognize the ways of lack much more easily.

- It gives you an ideal tool to hold on to what you have and what you hold dear.

Respect keeps the flow of abundance, of love in all its forms, in balance.

Respect is the way to hold onto the amount that you have. Not out of fear, because then you'll stop the flow of energy, but out of love. By respecting everything around you, money, power and love keep flowing! Respect is underestimated by many. People say "I do respect everything!" But in daily life, respect is often conditional. People very often respect others only for what they have accomplished, for what they stand for in politics, in business, or whatever. The surprise is that respect literally has to be unconditional at all times. Respect is all-embracing.

People tend to think lightly about this. But respect really deserves a central place in our lives and in the way we behave toward others. We are talking about respecting every form of energy:

- The energy of living beings
- The energy of money, power and love in every form
- The energy of every venture

Respecting living beings, people and animals of every shape and size. People... even if they have a totally unorthodox way of thinking, behave differently, and have different values than you do. Maybe you think, "okay, I'll do that," and from that moment on you think everything's okay and you don't dare to offer any form of criticism. But that has nothing to do with respect. That way of thinking leads to disinterest, indifference, and often forgetting your own values. Respecting someone means that you are able to honor them as a person even if they have ideas or values that you don't agree with. If that's the case, you have every right to say so and make clear what you think. Otherwise you wouldn't respect yourself.

Respect for money, power and love is reflected in virtually every aspect of our lives. Thanking the company that pays your salary is a powerful form of respect. Being happy with every cent that comes your way, no matter how, is showing respect. Paying someone in an honorable way, not indifferently—without bravado and without shame—is a form of respect for the energy of money. Whether you're paying your rent or leaving a tip in a restaurant, it's all about the attention and the measure of respect with which you do it. Respecting money also applies to savings or investments. Not enjoying your savings is a lack of respect. Not taking action when the market is in decline is a lack of respect. Respect also means daring to take action when money, power and love threaten to slip through your fingers.

Respecting power has to do with daring to allow the inner strength to come out. It's also about being happy when others have found their inner strength. Respect for power is also trusting the power itself, and daring not to be manipulative. Respect for power also means knowing the value of your health and your body, and treating them with respect.

Respect for love... your friends, your partner, love for your work, love for your house, your environment, and your country. Having respect for love means respecting the love you share with someone or something. It also means respecting the relationship that others share. You don't start a relationship with someone if you know that they are already in a relationship or have a steady partner; otherwise, you're not respecting the other person's relationship and you won't recognize your right to a genuine and sincere relationship! Trying to steal other peoples' clients is clearly a lack of respect. That is only logical; you would go after other people's clients only if you were focused on lack. Or are you afraid there won't be enough for you?

Respect is also relevant in every venture. A venture is not only a business or a project; everything you undertake falls into that category. From that point of view, it's clear that even a relationship, the desire to have a child, or building a home are all ventures. A venture is actually a spiritual process of creating something out of love, with your full attention.

The flow of money, power and love will be maintained if you take full responsibility for everything you undertake. That means you take yourself and whatever you undertake very seriously. Respect comes into your life as soon as you do things without indifference, replacing it with love and attention!

Respect is also an important factor in your interaction with others when it comes to money, power and love. You now know that money, power and love are not factors that just happen to appear in your life out of nowhere or disappear "by chance." You also know that walking the roads of abundance, or rather not walking the roads of lack, is a process of personal growth. That process can't be forced or stopped. That's why it's called a process of growth! Respect the personal path of others, no matter what they actually say and do. There is no good or bad; there's only growth and experience.

Helping and teaching about the natural laws of money, power and love is the nicest thing you can do, with respect for the process in which others find themselves and the choices they make.

FREQUENTLY ASKED QUESTIONS

Is there a difference between power and force?

Is there a difference between real strength and power?
Not really. Power is the consequence if you allow your inner strength to unfold. Both strength and power are necessary to be able to lead your life and also to support others leading theirs, and you also need them to be able to do the nice things in life.

Some people have a need for power, which has nothing to do with real strength but is a result of fear and is sometimes connected to feelings of superiority. This form of power is not genuine but encourages a lack of integrity as well as it encourages corruption. The challenge is to stimulate the power within yourself and within others without taking advantage of that power.

How do you recognize a flow problem?

That can easily be recognized from the external characteristics such as: complaining, forcing an opinion or project, blaming others, thoughts of running short, and attaching a lot of importance to networking. You'll recognize it from chaos. Chaos and disturbance in relations, in finance and ailing health.

How do you know if you are starting a project from a healthy basis or from fear?

If the project fills you with love, instead of fanaticism. If it goes smoothly, instead of your having to force everything. If it gives you more power than it takes to make it succeed. If in your spare time you think about your project and smile, if it feels good without your feeling stress and heart palpitations. If you face little opposition. If you don't have to invent detours to get people to support your plans and you don't have to lure them. If you don't have to play off the greed, or fear or lack in others. If you leave all this behind, you'll literally fill a project with love!

How do I harmonize the practical application of money power love with the principle of letting go?

Over the years, the idea of letting go has been interpreted in different ways. If you say often enough that you want to let go of everything, you can be sure that the cosmos will grant your wish. Letting go actually means letting go of your attachment to a particular result. Being focused on results means fear, but you can also be doing something because it gives you joy. Letting go implies you're not greedy or fearful. A person who has no attachment to the outer status of money, power and love does everything from love and joy! That doesn't mean that you should avoid any form of contact with this energy or cut off your contact with it. That's only avoiding your responsibilities. Money power love means that you dare to start a relationship with money and power and love, that you connect with the flow without allying yourself with the outer form and without becoming fearful of losing it, without greed, without an ego. It's also important to know that you can detach yourself from something only if you were first attached to it. You can release something only after you've had it.

What about investing in the stock market? Is that okay with this method and why is one person more successful at it than another?
Investing is fine using this method. If we really consider the natural laws of money power love, it's only logical that it will work according to these laws. Investing, in whatever, is one of the challenges in our goal of evaluating the laws of money power love. When you invest, you not only invest money but also power and love. Thus, the first question you have to ask yourself is whether the company or project you want to invest in is worth the investment of your money, power and love? Do you feel love for this company? Are their values and goals the same as yours? If the company or organization truly meets your standards and if their goals are like yours, you've already won the moment you invest. You'll have been given the chance, by means of your investment, to give the company a boost and to share your ideas with those around you.

This also explains why investors of the first hour do much better than the "followers." If a country undergoes a disaster or the economy takes a dip, there comes a moment when a select group of people are prepared to take the lead. This group of people know they are taking a great risk, but for them it's not about money (they most likely already have that in large quantities); it's about accepting responsibility. For the country, for each other, for the inhabitants. These people gather their courage and start to invest. The rest of the country looks on in anticipation, holding their breath, to see what the stock market will do. If things get better, that's when the middle group dares to step in. This middle group also has noble ideas, but lacks that extra bit of courage. The first group that took the initiative is giving the middle group the courage to overcome their fear and do the same. The rest of the country looks on, waiting in anticipation, holding their breath, to see what the market will do. Finally, the last group follows, the masses. This last group doesn't have any clear noble motives that involve money, power and love, but mainly looks at performance in the past, in the present, and what it might be in the future. The last group considers only the "money" aspect and what they can get out of it. As you now know, this attitude has nothing to do with sharing, only with taking. This group will most likely be the first to withdraw if profits are disappointing, because their motive for investing was not love and thoughts of abundance, but just the opposite - fear and thoughts of lack.

Every investment works according to the three natural laws of money power and love. Even if you decide to invest in a third world country, you can decide to do so out of love for its people, for the country and for the business or organization you're investing in. That way you'll always be a winner, even if the profit or price might be disappointing. Investing is sharing!

Why is it that some companies do so well even if they don't seem to serve any good cause other than doing business?

The term "good cause" is interesting. A good cause is actually serving your highest ideal, the thing for which you can muster all your love. If, for instance, you look at the largest and most successful software company in the world and you see the CEO and creator giving a speech in which he talks about his newest product, you'll see someone who's informing his audience about his newborn, about his "child." That person isn't selling a product; he's selling pure love. Of course we're talking here about people just like you and me, and they too will know or have known times when money, power and love are totally in balance and times when that was less the case. A company's or organization's intention is more often love than you may think.

Do you always have to receive an energy exchange from your work, or can it be a vocation?

We realize that many people nowadays differentiate between the work they do to earn a living and work done as a calling or vocation. The thought that lurks behind this is that work done as a calling doesn't have to be paid for. "After all, it's his calling." The division between work and a calling is an illusion. All work ought to be a calling. With every form of work we should respect the flow of money, power and love. Otherwise there will come a time, in the long run, when there's a group of people who work only for money and another who perform their work as a calling. In today's society, it seems like the more a job is related to spirituality, to the divine aspect, the worse the pay. Materiality of every kind in the form of television, shows, partying, even to extremes like drugs and sex, are all well paid and cost even more of the average person's budget. Spiritual teachers, churches, and social workers are paid reluctantly. We feel like we have to, sometimes out of habit or because of nagging guilt. That says an awful lot about today's values; after all, what you give attention grows and what you ignore doesn't. In fact, by maintaining the imaginary division between work and a calling, you're giving attention to the professions that are there "for money" and ignoring the callings in life. There are also farmers, bakers, artists, and dentists who perform their skills and crafts with honor, from a feeling that this is their highest ideal in life. Having a vocation or calling and a healthy energy exchange go together wonderfully!

If money power love is one energy, why do kids who are born with an abundance of money, power and love often have so many problems?

If we look at the privileged children of the wealthy, of movie stars or industrialists, we often see that things frequently go wrong. Many see such children as privileged. However, that's not always how the children themselves experience it. The attention, the power, and the large amounts of money are often too much to handle. Often the level of consciousness that's needed to take full responsibility is lacking.

Money, power and love are nothing but different forms of the same thing!

These children have never learned how to handle so much energy! They haven't learned how to generate it; they haven't consciously lived through the process of learning to work with energy with their parents.

I can accept this method, but I still have a problem with the fact that people with lots of money can suddenly change.

When somebody in your surroundings suddenly has a lot of money (or power, or love), you'll see who and what that person really is. It may shock you, but everything you see was already there to begin with! For that matter, you can truly thank money, because there is nothing else that makes people so honest and true to themselves! People can truly blossom if they have more money. They search for more depth in their lives, and because of their newfound material welfare they can devote more time to their relations and friends. On the other hand there are also people who change, but not for the better.

If it is all one energy and nobody becomes poorer because it's actually an exchange of energy, it must be okay to ask whatever you want for your services and products?

Exchange means that you have to deliver something that is of equal value to what you receive. There are therapists and managers who earn a low hourly rate, and there are those who earn a high hourly rate. If you choose to charge a high hourly rate, which means a larger exchange of energy, you have to deliver what was paid for! In practice that is generally the case, but not always. Managers of large companies and organizations, professional athletes, actors, and musicians often do deliver that quality, that exchange, in the first years, but at a certain point they stop. When you become successful, it's a challenge to keep respecting the exchange of energy. Every form of exchange, whether it's money, power, or love, demands our full attention and respect. Thus, the answer is yes, if you're able to deliver proportionately, there isn't any maximum.

I invest so much in love and still it doesn't help. How is that possible?

There is no such thing as investing in love. You already are love. What you can do is invest in yourself and share that with others. Then you're sharing with your surroundings what you are and above all who you are. What we often see with people who "invest in love" is that they mainly end up sharing sacrifice and their lack of love for themselves with their surroundings. To be perfectly honest, no one loves or respects a lack of love for oneself or sacrifice, although there are enough people who fall for those qualities. But a relationship built on that basis will never be satisfying. You can build a beautiful, loving relationship by becoming what you would like to see in another! Work on yourself, enjoy, allow yourself a life of abundance, and start sharing that with others.

But aren't there people who never had a chance?

We don't all get the same start in life, that's a fact. It may seem like one person gets a head start in life, while someone else has to realize love and abundance from an utterly miserable situation. One person grows up in a home with an abusive father and a mother who drinks, and someone else knows only a protective environment with plenty on the table and an expensive car in the driveway. The first situation we quickly label deprived and the other fortunate. These labels are misleading. It's an inner struggle that seems lost from the start. That inner feeling of not making the mark can permanently retard a person's growth. Whatever your start in life, every person has a chance. It's about freeing yourself from the feeling that you have to prove yourself or the feeling that you're a failure or inferior, without denying or disavowing your origins.

We all have just as many chances, they're just different! The trap in which most of us fall into is to blame someone else for the situation we're in and to constantly use it as an excuse for our actions. Even if it's true that you didn't get a good start in life, by dwelling on it you won't change it. In fact, by dwelling on it you only re-enforce your own situation and deny yourself any and all opportunities! *Whatever you focus on will grow.*

CONCLUSION

Small doors sometimes lead to large spaces, and every big journey begins with a first step. Large things start small... Bill Gates, the head of Microsoft, started with an idea and a floppy disk in a garage. Steve Jobs, the founder of Apple, the most innovative computer (and music) company, started with nothing but an idea... Nelson Mandela only had a vision and managed to share an amazing amount of power and love. Gloria Estefan started with nothing, and it was her inner power and her love for life and the music that brought her to where she is now. The creator of Harry Potter was a single mother on welfare who wrote her first book in the corner of a small cafe because she didn't have enough money for electricity or heating at home. Power and love drove her and enabled her to start the flow.

We, too, can take into account the principles—the laws of nature—of money power and love. When we purchase products, go out to eat, start new relationships or maintain old friendships, we can do it in a way that maintains the balance in the energy of money, power and love. That means we prefer to associate with people, companies, and organizations where this balance is present and where it's obvious that they live and work from this level of respect. We also make our important life decisions based on these three laws of nature. Are money, power and love in balance? Are all three forms being respected? Will this plan start the flow, and are receiving, using and passing on in balance? And we have to ask ourselves whether it's fully in harmony with our life, with our highest ideals.

You, the reader, are now able to look at the energy of money power love in a totally different way and to handle it differently, more responsibly. Knowledge of these laws of nature allows you to improve your health, your love relationships, your friendships, and your financial situation. Make the world an even better place!

And remember that it's not about how much money, power and love you have, but about the quality and balance of the whole!

Reflection

It has been our experience that people who live their lives in harmony with these laws of nature and have reached a measure of balance also incorporate moments of inner quiet, reflection, and healing into their lives. Life, particularly in accordance with this method, is a great spiritual adventure, and we believe that inner support is always welcome. Any technique that leads to inner peace and a process of spiritual growth, healing, and new insights is appropriate. Anything from deep prayer to meditation, yoga, shin-do or Reiki. Personally, we use the original Reiki techniques and shin-do® for this. Our daily reflections ward us every day with new insights and continually enable us to stay with our "inner truth."

THE AUTHORS

As metaphysical and spiritual counselors, Bas Buis and Sunny Nederlof inspire their students and course participants in the field of growth, healing, and inner wisdom. They are the founders of the renowned Nederlof Centrum and the Reiki-Institute in the Netherlands. They live and teach in the Netherlands and in France and are regular guests in many different countries.

They are both Usui Master in the tradition of Usui Shiki Ryoho and Reiki Ryoho and are the founders of the Shin-Do® method, the Money Power Love method and the Auratouch® Professional Healer Program.

For more information:

Nederlof Centrum
Web site: www.nederlofcentrum.com
E-mail: info@nederlofcentrum.com

NOTES